All Work & All Play

All Work & All Play
A Life in the Outrageous World of Sports

Jim Hunt

John Wiley & Sons Canada, Ltd.

National Library of Canada Cataloguing in Publication Data

Hunt, Jim, 1926-
   All work and all play : a life in the outrageous world of sports / Jim Hunt.

Includes index.
ISBN-13 978-0-470-83552-4
ISBN-10 0-470-83552-4

1. Hunt, Jim, 1926-   2. Sportswriters—Canada—Biography.   I. Title.

GV742.42.H85A3 2005   070.4'49796'092   C2005-903372-X

Production Credits:
Cover and interior text design: Adrian So
Printer: Printcrafters

Front Cover Photos: Clockwise from top right: Jim Hunt with Rocky Marciano; Jim Hunt with Mickey Mantle; Jim Hunt with Stan Musial (All courtesy of Jim Hunt)
Back Cover Photo: Jim Hunt with Joe Kapp (Courtesy of Jim Hunt)

John Wiley & Sons Canada, Ltd.
6045 Freemont Blvd.
Mississauga, Ontario
L5R 4J3

Printed in Canada
10 9 8 7 6 5 4 3 2 1

For Caroline and our family

Table of Contents

Foreword   ix

Acknowledgments   xiii

Introduction   1

1 Lunch with Marilyn:
Working at the *Star*   5

2 What a Riot:
Rocket Richard   19

3 They Did Have Glory Years:
The Toronto Argos   29

4 Grand National Drunk:
The Grey Cup   43

5 The Greatest Athlete:
Muhammad Ali   57

6 The Greatest Games:
The Canada–Russia Hockey Series   69

Table of Contents

7 Fab Six:
Howe, Beliveau, Hull, Orr, Gretzky, Lemieux 81

8 The Legends:
From Lionel Conacher to Northern Dancer 107

9 No Friend of the Maple Leafs:
Pal Hal 119

10 The Super Bowls:
So Rarely Super 129

11 Dopes and Hopes:
Canada in the Olympics 141

12 Covering Baseball:
Maris, Mantle, and the Babe 151

13 From the Elite to Defeat:
Baseball in Canada 161

14 Covering Golf:
Palmer, Nicklaus, and Me 173

15 Media Scrum:
Working with Dunnell, Gross, Beddoes, et al. 191

Index 208

About the Author 218

Foreword
by Steve Simmons

ONLY ONCE HAVE I seen Jim Hunt rendered speechless.

He and I, along with David Shoalts of *The Globe and Mail*, were driving in a rental car during Super Bowl week in Miami, in 1989, having just eaten fabulously at the famous Joe's Stone Crab restaurant. We were having the only kind of conversation you can have with Jim—loud, louder, and always funny—when we were waved off the highway at a police blockade with bright lights flashing.

What are we stopping for?" Shaky screamed, which is close to his regular decible level. (Shaky is a nickname Hunt picked up in college because, he claims, as a goaltender he was less than stellar and let in more shots than he stopped.) Being the driver and a naïve Canadian, I got out of the car and walked toward the officer to ask for directions to our hotel. The officer didn't flinch. Over a megaphone the size of New Jersey, but not quite as loud as Jim, he blasted at me: "Get the *@+&* back in your car unless you want to die."

And so I did. Quickly and quietly. We drove from the roadblock through parts of Overtown, running red lights, not sure where we were going, hearing the sound of gunfire, not fully comprehending that we were in the middle of a full-blown civic riot. Not once on the ride did anyone speak.

Have you ever had a friend, or a colleague at work, that you could listen to all day long? One who sees life as an anecdote, who finds a story in everything, who speaks with such unbridled passion, and sometimes crazy enthusiasm, that you don't want to miss a single syllable of their stream of consciousness?

That's what it was like to work with or around Jim. We had a front seat on a most enjoyable class act, but we may not have taken the time to appreciate everything about him: where he has been, to whom he has spoken, the way in which he relates the tales that have been his life.

A number of years ago over dinner, my oldest son, who wasn't very old at the time, asked the kind of question grade one kids tend to ask.

"Dad," he said, "who's your best friend at work?"

I paused for a moment and then answered, "Jim Hunt."

"Jim Hunt?" he said. "Isn't he that old guy?"

"No," I corrected him. "He's just about the youngest man I know."

Foreword

At the time, Jim was 70 going on 16. He was still working years after we organized his retirement party. He is beyond 70 now but remains the oldest, big, hunched-over kid I've ever known, a giant of a man with a giant voice so full of folly and laughter and stories and adventure.

Jim doesn't just tell a good story, he writes a good story, too. And now, finally, we have the opportunity to read all about Jim's experiences in this book.

Those of us who love sport know Muhammad Ali from dusty film clips and recent documentaries and motion pictures and the plethora of terrific books written about him. Jim was there the night he knocked out Sonny Liston with the so-called phantom punch.

Most of us know Mickey Mantle from old reels of Yankee memories and more recently from Billy Crystal's movie *61**. Jim interviewed Mickey in the dugout at Yankee Stadium.

Everyone in Canada over the age of 40 knows precisely where he or she was when Paul Henderson scored the most famous goal in hockey history, in 1972. Jim does, too. He was in Moscow, chronicling the historic moment.

We know the stories, he lived them. He did what the best journalists, whether in radio or in print, always do: He took us to the ballpark or the Grey Cup or the Super Bowl right alongside him. We could hear the crowd and smell the mustard. We always knew what the events looked like and tasted like. And he always replayed things for us with his own unique signature and voice.

Foreword

Travelling with Jim is an experience. He makes for great company, but I have to say that he is technologically challenged. We were flying executive class on Air Canada to cover the Stanley Cup Playoffs. The headsets were passed around and a movie came on the screen. Jim struggled to plug his headset into the little holes. I did it for him. He couldn't set the volume dial. I helped him. He couldn't find the channel. I helped him again, sort of. Then the movie—*Three Men and a Baby*—started rolling. The first several minutes are a party scene and all you hear is music. Then the first words were spoken. If Jim is loud speaking normally, he is something else entirely with headphones on.

"This movie's in French," he screamed out.

The entire plane cracked up.

"Uh, Jim," I said, turning to him. "That's channel one for English, channel two for French."

One last Hunt story before you read his. During the 1998 playoffs in Edmonton, Jim had the temerity to suggest in print that Wayne Gretzky had grown too large for the Alberta capital and it was time for him to be traded. The post-column reaction was wild and personal. Local radio shows were calling him a crazy old man. With all the controversy swirling around him, Shaky just smiled and basked in the attention.

Two months later, on a day that changed hockey forever, Gretzky was traded to the Los Angeles Kings.

Turns out Jim Hunt wasn't such a crazy old man after all.

—*Steve Simmons is a columnist with the* Toronto Sun.

Acknowledgments

I OWE A DEBT of gratitude to many people for helping me with this book. I wrote the first 10 chapters many years ago but was unable to find a publisher at the time. The manuscript might have remained in a drawer in my den if not for Perry Lefko, a colleague of mine at the *Toronto Sun*. Perry put me in touch with Arnold Gosewich, an agent who had represented him on some of his books. It was Arnold who offered me encouragement to complete the project.

My grandson, Ben Hunt, contributed the computer expertise that I lacked. My wife, Caroline, helped with the editing. And Don Bastian added the finishing touches.

I would also like to thank Harold Barkley, a good friend and a great photographer, who traveled with me on many assignments.

Thank you all. Without you, it wouldn't have happened.

JIM HUNT

Introduction

IN NEARLY 50 YEARS in journalism, I have been fortunate to meet, talk to, and write about hundreds of interesting people, primarily in the world of sports. My beat was mainly Canada but included the United States and beyond. I covered everything from boxing to baseball, hockey, golf, and "Canada's National Drunk"—the Grey Cup, and athletes from Mickey Mantle to Maurice Richard to Muhammad Ali to Gordie Howe and Bobby Orr to Arnold Palmer and Tiger Woods. This book is my way of sharing with readers some of these experiences and stories.

I joined the *Toronto Star* in 1948, a graduate of the newly established journalism course at the University of Western Ontario; in fact, I was a member of the first graduating class. I decided early in life that I loved the newspaper business.

Introduction

My brothers and I, during our teenage years, published a newspaper called the *St. Clair Weekly Bugle*. We donated the profits, which were rather small, to wartime charity. I also worked for the *Sarnia Observer* during the summer while I was going to university.

My initial experience at the *Star* was in general reporting, then to Queen's Park as a member of the press gallery. In 1953 I transferred to the sports department under the legendary Milt Dunnell.

I moved to the *Toronto Star Weekly* as sports editor in 1961. My assignments included Olympic Games, major golf tournaments, and baseball spring training. In 1967, I moved to radio station CKEY as news and sports director. One of my most important assignments included covering both the 1972 and '74 series against the Russians for CKEY as well as for the now defunct News Radio National Network and CBS radio in the U.S. I also covered the Montreal Olympics. I was hired by the *Toronto Sun* in 1983 as a sports columnist and still write a regular column once a week. Also at that time I was a regular panelist on CTV's *Canada AM*. Starting in 1991, I spent 10 years as co-host of *Prime Time Sports*, a nationally syndicated radio program on The Fan 590 and am currently doing some morning segments for the station.

Two things stand out for me as I look back on these years from my vast age and eminence. One is that there is no more outrageous arena in which to work than sports. Competitiveness seems to create the weirdest characters with the

Introduction

strangest lives doing the most eccentric things. The other is that covering sports never really felt like work.

In the more than 50 years I have spent in this business, there have been many changes. When I started, stories were written on a typewriter, transcribed and sent by telegraph operator. The telegraph people were not always objective. I was covering a game between the Argos and Ottawa and my operator made changes in my copy because he felt I was favouring the Argonauts. He was right; I was. Sometimes the copy did not even wind up at your own paper. My brother Don and I were once covering the Masters in 1959. Don was working for the *Toronto Telegram*, and I was working for the *Star*. My copy wound up at the *Telegram*. They just phoned the *Star* and told them to come over and pick it up. I guess they weren't very impressed with the story. Now, of course, everyone in the business uses computers. I write a story on my laptop and send it over the phone to a computer in the newspaper's office. Even my method has become outdated by the invention of e-mail. When it works, it's wonderful, but there are times when the computer acts up. I was at a Super Bowl at Stanford Stadium in California. I couldn't get my story through to the office in Toronto. The computer geek (and they are different from the rest of us) said the problem was too much noise. He suggested I find a quiet place to send the story. I would like to know where you would find one in a stadium with 70,000 screaming football fans. I found myself dictating the story just as they did back

Introduction

in the good old days before computers. I'm sure the business has changed for the better. You can write a story anywhere in the world, and it can be sent directly into the newspaper's system. Technology is not the only change in the newspaper business. Maybe it's old age, but I think we had a lot more fun in the old days. Perhaps because we drank a little too much, but we always did get the work finished.

All through my years as a sports reporter, I had to pinch myself to see if this was real. I seem to have had the unusual luck of landing in some kind of warp zone where my work was play. Perfect.

1

Lunch with Marilyn:
Working at the *Star*

I REALLY DIDN'T KNOW what to expect on a sunny May morning in 1948 when I walked into the city room of the *Toronto Star*, the biggest newspaper in Canada.

I had just graduated in journalism from the University of Western Ontario in London. Alex Givens, the paper's executive editor who hired me, had a word of advice. "Don't tell anyone, especially Tommy Lytle, the city editor, that you studied journalism at university," he said. "They don't think too much of journalism schools around here."

Lytle may well have been the best newsman in Canada at the time. He also struck fear into the hearts of every young reporter on the staff.

One day he yelled across the newsroom, "Hunt, get a photographer and go to Aurora."

Chapter 1

I made the mistake of asking him why.

"You think you're a newspaperman," he hollered. "Find out."

When the photographer and I arrived in Aurora, then a sleepy town 30 miles north of Toronto, the main street was on fire. This is why Lytle sent us—to cover the fire—but he did not want to tell us. He felt we would find out soon enough, and of course we did.

The next five years, spent as a reporter for the *Star*, were the most exciting of my life. The *Star* and the *Toronto Telegram* were in a life-and-death struggle for circulation. I still find some of the things we did hard to believe. For example, covering Marilyn Bell's swim across Lake Ontario brought out the best and the worst in both papers. The *Star* had an exclusive deal with the 16-year-old swimmer—or so they thought. They even had boats hired to keep reporters from the *Telegram* away. But that did not stop the *Telegram* from trying to get their story.

The word "journalist" was not one heard in the newsroom of either the *Star* or the *Tely*. Journalist was a broad term, encompassing all writers. We were reporters, working in the newsroom, and proud of it. Our jobs, as young reporters, involved more than reporting on events.

Among the other jobs given to young reporters was picking up pictures of accident victims. Come back without a picture of the man or woman who had been killed and you'd come back to no job.

One night early in my career at the *Star* we got a report that a streetcar had hit a car and three young men had burned to death in the crash.

I was sent to their home in North Toronto to pick up pictures of the three brothers who had been killed. As soon as I got to the door I realized the family didn't know their sons had been killed. I told them I wanted a picture and they naturally wondered why.

You had to think fast on your feet for this job. I suggested they'd been promoted in their jobs. That didn't work since they were waiters at a tavern across from the racetrack.

"The tavern is running an ad and they want to use your sons' pictures in it," I told the father.

He bought the story. He got the pictures of his sons out of a family album. I had them in my hands when the phone rang.

It was a reporter from *The Globe and Mail* who told them their three sons had been killed in the accident. The mother, who had answered the phone, screamed and then fainted. The father picked it up and then turned to me and started to yell: "My boys are dead. They were alive when you came in here."

He grabbed a butcher knife and started to chase me. I dropped the pictures and ran out the door to a waiting cab.

Another cab drew up and a reporter from the *Telegram* got out. He was at the door before I could warn him. The door opened and the father gave him a solid punch in the mouth.

Chapter 1

I got back to the office and told the night editor what had happened.

"Why don't you go back and try again?" he asked.

I replied there was no way I was going. I liked my job but loved my life an awful lot better.

They say you've never really made it as a reporter 'til you've been punched, sued, and thrown in jail. I qualify for all three.

I was covering a strike at the Penman's plant in Paris (Ontario, not France). Late one afternoon I was watching the picket line when an organizer for the union was arrested. I tried to get close to the cruiser when the two policemen grabbed me and put me in the car. On the way to the station, I told the police I was a reporter for the *Star*. They obviously thought I was a member of the union. They put me in a cell and locked the door. It's an experience I'm not anxious to repeat.

I asked what I was charged with and got no reply. Finally a provincial police inspector came to my cell and told me I was charged with obstructing police.

After a couple of hours, Eric Cole, the *Star* photographer who was working with me, put up $50 bail and I was let out.

The next morning my picture, behind bars, was on the front page of *The Globe and Mail*. I phoned my mother, then living in London, and told her not to worry about her son being in jail. It was just part of the job.

The next morning I was ordered to come home for a meeting with Harry Hindmarsh, the *Star*'s publisher. Ernest Hemingway, who worked for the *Star* in the 1920s, once compared working for Hindmarsh to being in the Prussian Army with a bad general. Pretty accurate. I really didn't know what to expect when I was ushered into Hindmarsh's office. I thought the worst thing that could happen was that I'd be fired.

Hindmarsh told me to sit down. "My wife told me this morning that she can't understand how a nice looking young man like you can get in so much trouble," he said.

He called in Norm James, the *Star*'s senior photographer. "Go over to the window and look out," he commanded me. I wasn't sure what he had in mind. Perhaps he was going to throw me onto King Street. I guess he just wanted to see what I would look like with the light from the window behind me. "Make him look like the young Lindbergh," Hindmarsh told the photographer, referring to the pilot who was the first to fly the Atlantic solo.

James took me out to the parking lot, had me gaze to the sky, and took the picture. The *Star* ran the photo in that afternoon's paper alongside a story of mine. Underneath was a brief biography and this rather strange sentence: "At university he was known as the hardest man to pick a fight with." I was not a fighter in college, but I certainly did not back down from a scrap. The last time I was in a brawl, I threw a punch, missed and put my fist through a window in a hotel room. I have no idea who was the source of the quote. In those days the *Star* didn't worry about such things.

The provincial police indicated they'd be willing to drop the charge. The *Star*, who never passed up a chance to embarrass the Tory government, wanted no part of it. They were determined I'd go to trial. They hired prominent Bay Street lawyer T.N. Phelan to defend me. It convinced me that if you're ever in trouble with the law, make sure you get a good lawyer.

I was acquitted without putting in a defence, though the magistrate did allow me to have my say in court. It wasn't every day a big name lawyer from Toronto appeared in his court and the magistrate loved every minute of it.

I hate to think of what might have happened if I didn't have the *Star* resources behind me. A $50-a-week reporter was not going to be able to afford a lawyer with the reputation of my counsel. I probably would have been convicted. Technically, I did obstruct the police, the crime with which I was charged.

I'm convinced that you have to be lucky, as well as good, to hack it as a reporter on a metropolitan daily. I had more than my share of good luck. If I had been home in bed, as I've been for most Friday nights in my life, I wouldn't have run into the biggest story I've ever covered.

In the summer of 1949, I was living on the Toronto Islands, which, before the politicians got into the act, was as interesting a place as I've ever lived.

I had driven my girlfriend Caroline, who's now been my wife for more than 50 years, to her sister's home in Port Credit. I drove back to the city and parked my car in a lot across the street from where the water taxis were docked.

I went into a diner for a cup of coffee to wait for the next boat. A couple of minutes later someone came in screaming, "There's a big boat on fire."

I ran out and the sky was red with flames. I raced the half mile to the dock where the ship was burning. It was the *Noronic*, a ship I had sailed aboard to Port Arthur when I was a youngster. It seemed like losing an old friend to see her go up in flames. The *Noronic* docked in my hometown of Sarnia every Saturday on her way to the head of the lakes, and for the kids it was a big day. We dove for money tossed by the passengers. The captain was a friend of my father. He allowed me to take the wheel of the *Noronic*, at the time the biggest passenger ship on the lakes. It was an experience a six-year-old was unlikely to forget.

The fire trucks had not yet arrived when I got to the ship. The top deck was enveloped in flames. It was a scene of bedlam as passengers clambered down ropes to escape from the ship.

I raced to a telephone booth to call the office. "The *Noronic*'s on fire at the waterfront," I shouted into the receiver.

The night editor, a crusty veteran by the name of Fred Troyer, wasn't impressed.

"I haven't heard the fire alarms," he said. "Hunt, you must be drunk." Then he hung up.

I called him back a couple of minutes later and by then the fire trucks were on their way. This time he believed me. "I can't find any photographers," he said.

The reason was that someone was shooting up the police station in Alliston, a town 62 miles from Toronto. The *Star* had sent a platoon of reporters and photographers to cover the event. That was the way they did things in those wonderful, wacky days.

I was supposed to be with the crew in Alliston, but I talked my way out of the assignment, on the grounds I was hung over from a stag the night before. What I didn't tell the city editor was that I had a date that night.

The first *Star* reporter to join me at the scene was Scotty Humeniuk, a classmate at Western. The cab driver who brought him to the waterfront had a movie camera with him. Scotty, whom I gather had a few drinks under his belt, made like Cecil B. DeMille directing the cab-driver-turned-movie-cameraman. He was so busy directing he fell backwards into the harbour. He was fished out by the police and joined a group of survivors in a boat bringing them to safety.

Lunch with Marilyn

It was one humorous moment in a night of tragedy. I was standing beside Nelson Quarrington, the veteran cameraman of the *Telegram*, when he took a picture of a man walking down the gangplank, smoking a cigar and carrying his briefcase as the ship burned behind him. It won Quarrington a National Newspaper Award.

A photographer for *The Globe and Mail* was also standing there. For some reason he didn't take the picture. Anyone who was there that horrible night can understand why. Watching over 100 people burning to death in front of your eyes was enough to make even a veteran newsman forget what he was supposed to be doing.

Besides, his bosses at *The Globe and Mail* had decided they wouldn't hold the press for him anyway. The city editor who made the decision was an old Ottawa hand who thought fires were beneath his paper. He was soon on the first train back to the nation's capital.

I still hadn't been to bed when I got to the *Star* newsroom. "How would you like to go to Detroit with a trainload of survivors?" the city editor said.

I knew it wasn't a suggestion but an order. I went to Detroit on the train, filed my story, and finally, 48 hours after I got up, fell into bed.

I got my reward the next day. The editor asked how I'd feel about flying home. I thought it was a great idea since I'd never been on an airplane. Since then I've flown all over the world, but that flight on an old DC-3 from Windsor to

Chapter 1

Toronto is one I'll never forget.

Jack Kennedy and I had one thing in common. We both had lunch with Marilyn Monroe. All I had was lunch, in 1951, but I have been dining out on it for 50 years.

I actually got to meet Marilyn by accident when she was in Niagara Falls making a movie. The senior writer assigned to the story had annoyed the producer with his stories that appeared in the *Star* and he was banned from the set. I was sitting in the newsroom when Bordon Spears, the city editor, asked if I would like to have lunch with Marilyn Monroe. At the time she was a young actress who was notorious for having been photographed in the buff. She appeared in calendars that were in half the gas stations in the U.S.

I don't remember much of what Marilyn said during lunch, however I do recall she had on a low-cut dress and spoke in that throaty voice that was soon to be her trademark. The photographer I was working with asked if Marilyn would agree to pose for some pictures. She agreed to meet us in her suite later in the afternoon. We showed up at the appointed hour but there was no answer when we rapped at the door. A bellhop told us we were wasting our time as she was in there with "the ballplayer." Of course, it was Joe DiMaggio, who eventually became her husband. At the time he was still married, and in the 1950s it would never do to have a star shacked up with a married man. The morality of Hollywood has changed since the 1950s. Now if movie stars have affairs no one really seems to care, especially their studios, which make the most of it for publicity purposes.

You meet such interesting people in this business. One thing a young boy who grew up in Sarnia never expected was to have a gin and tonic with the Queen of England. I went home one June day in 1976 and found an invitation in the mail from Her Majesty, Queen Elizabeth II. She was inviting James Richard Hunt to have drinks aboard the Royal Yacht Britannia while she was in Montreal for the Olympics.

Hunt didn't have anything better to do that Sunday afternoon so he put on his best suit and the only white shirt he had with him in Montreal, borrowed a beat-up old Mustang, and drove to the dock where the royal yacht was berthed.

The gin was Plymouth and the bartenders on the Britannia poured strong ones. It's a dangerous game because protocol insists you can't leave, even to go to the head, till the Queen departs. You need willpower, strong kidneys, or preferably both.

You are also not supposed to quote anything the Queen says when you meet her. Actually, it wasn't much of a problem. She talked of her daughter Anne, who was a member of the British equestrian team at the Olympics. The Queen of England was just like any other proud parent, watching her daughter march in the parade that opened the Games.

When I think back on the wackiest things that happened to me as a reporter with the *Star*, this one goes to the top of the list.

It involves hockey legend Gordie Howe, who I was later to write about often when I switched to sports, and his buddy, Ted Lindsay.

The Red Wings were in Toronto in 1956 for a Stanley Cup Playoff game with the Leafs. The phone in the city room rang and I picked it up.

"If Howe and Lindsay show up for the game tonight I'm going to shoot them," the caller said and hung up.

I told Bill Drylie, the city editor. He had me call the police. I told them of the threatening phone call. I was assured they'd be keeping a careful eye on fans entering Maple Leaf Gardens that night.

I told Drylie what the police had said. "Why don't you see if you can smuggle a gun into the Gardens?" he said.

At first I thought he was kidding. I should have known better. Drylie wasn't much for kidding.

We agreed taking a real rifle into the Gardens might be a little too much. Besides, I'd already been arrested once and didn't much like the idea of going behind bars again.

So we compromised. John MacDonald, a sportswriter for the *Star*, volunteered to make a wooden mock-up of a gun. He'd put it into a gun case and no one would know the difference.

My wife was supposed to accompany me to the game but when I told her of the gun, she decided to stay home. I called Jack Brehl, a *Star* reporter, and asked if he'd like to go to the game. It was a hot ticket in those days (and it still is), and he needed no urging.

Star photographer Paul Smith and I picked Brehl up. It wasn't until we got to the parking lot and I got the gun case out of the trunk that my guest realized what was up. He grabbed his ticket and said he'd meet me in the seats.

I slung the gun case over my shoulder and walked through the lobby, past the ticket takers, to my seat in the blues.

I put the gun between my legs and sat back to enjoy the game. No one seemed to notice. After the game, which the Red Wings won, Lindsay skated around the rink pointing his hockey stick, as if it were a gun, at the crowd.

The *Star* ran the picture of me and the gun case on the front page the next day. It convinced me, if I ever doubted it, that you can get away with almost anything as long as you don't blink. As for the threat, we never found out if it was just a hoax, as many of them are.

It wasn't until I left the real world for the sports department that I completed my triple. I was sued and punched and probably deserved to be on both counts. These are

Chapter 1

stories that will have to wait for the chapter on the Argos, a team I covered from the penthouse to the outhouse and back to the top again.

2

What a Riot:
Rocket Richard

MARCH 17, 1955 IS A DAY that no one who was in the Montreal Forum will ever forget—one of the blackest in the history of hockey.

It was the night of the Richard hockey riots, an orgy of destruction set off when NHL president Clarence Campbell suspended the Rocket for the remainder of the regular season and the playoffs.

It's hard to imagine the suspension of Wayne Gretzky or Mario Lemieux inciting the fans in Los Angeles or Pittsburgh to do what the fans did inside and outside the Forum that St. Patrick's Day evening. But then no one, before or since, has stirred the passions of the fans the way the Rocket did. He had a charisma that has been matched by only a handful of athletes within the sporting world.

Chapter 2

The problem was that a French-Canadian star was being judged by an English-Canadian president of the league. It may well have been the beginning of the troubles that were to plague the province of Quebec for the next three decades.

Richard was suspended following an incident in Boston where he went berserk, attacking the Bruins' Hal Laycoe with his stick and then going after the linesman who had tried to restrain him. It was not the first time Richard had been involved in such an incident. The president felt he had little choice but to suspend him.

I covered the hearing in the NHL offices in Montreal for the *Toronto Star*. It may have been one of the biggest sports stories in the history of the city but the English-language papers didn't seem impressed. The *Gazette* chose to rely on Canadian Press. Baz O'Meara, the sports editor of the *Star*, phoned in occasionally from a nearby tavern but never made it to the hearing.

The reaction to Campbell's suspension of Richard for the rest of the season and the playoffs was immediate. I was in the NHL office in Montreal when the phone started to ring.

"If you show up at the game tomorrow, we'll kill you." He wanted to get Campbell but anyone who answered the phone got the message.

The Rocket couldn't believe it when told he was finished for the season. "It's impossible," he told coach Dick Irvin, who gave him the news. The Rocket stormed out of the Forum. Teammates said they'd never seen him so mad.

What a Riot

Newspaper reaction in Montreal was split along linguistic lines. The French papers condemned Campbell's decision. "Campbell has often lacked judgement," wrote Jacques Beauchamp in *Montreal Matin*. "The decision he handed down yesterday is simply revolting. It could ruin hockey in Montreal. Campbell has once again shown utter stupidity." This was typical of the reaction of the French press and the fans.

The English media and the owners of the other teams in the league lined up beside the president. "I am with the president 100 per cent and back him to the limit," said Conn Smythe, the owner of the Toronto Maple Leafs. "It shows that the NHL and hockey is bigger than its greatest star."

Campbell felt he had no choice but to go to the game with the Detroit Red Wings that night. The police felt the calls were the work of cranks and didn't suggest, let alone urge, the president to stay away. Campbell took his customary seat in the northwest corner of the rink. He was greeted with a chorus of boos, which was to be expected.

It wasn't until the teams had left the ice at the end of the first period that the trouble really started. First, two young men rushed towards Campbell and threw rotten tomatoes that splattered over the president and his secretary, who had accompanied him to the game. The president didn't even flinch. He was still sitting there when someone tossed a tear gas canister in his direction. The canister exploded and the smell of gas soon drifted through the Forum.

It was fortunate that it was between periods and most of the fans had left their seats to go to the refreshment stands. There might have been panic if fans, their eyes filled with tears from the tear gas, had fought to get to the exits.

The gas wafted up to the press box but we were advised to stay there and not rush for the doors. I phoned my boss, Milt Dunnell, the sports editor of the *Star*. "I've covered prison riots," I told him, "but I've never seen anything like this." It was a madhouse in the Forum. I have never seen anything like it, certainly in this country.

The police ordered the game halted, and under NHL rules it was forfeited to Detroit. The announcement was greeted with catcalls by the crowd. Soon they spilled out onto Ste-Catherine Street, where they were joined by hundreds who had gathered outside the Forum.

The mob raced up Ste-Catherine, the main street of Montreal, in an orgy of destruction. They smashed store windows and looted the contents, throwing them into the street. The damage was estimated at more than a million dollars, one of the worst riots in the history of the city.

Mayor Jean Drapeau blamed Campbell for the riot. He had told the president he shouldn't go to the game. A Montreal city councillor went even further. He wanted the president charged, claiming his presence had "provoked the riot."

The president could be accused of many things but cowardice was not one of them. "If I hadn't showed up I would have been giving in to the mob," said Campbell. He went to his grave believing he was right and I'm inclined to agree with him.

The next night the Rocket appeared on television from the Canadiens dressing room in the Forum. He appealed to the people of Montreal to accept his suspension as he was prepared to do.

The populace heeded the plea from their biggest sports hero. There were hundreds mingling outside the Forum for the game that Saturday with the New York Rangers. Campbell, at the urging of the police, didn't attend. Hundreds of media from all over North America, quite a contrast to the handful who had been there two nights before, were in the press box.

They wound up with no story except for a routine hockey game. It was just another Saturday night in the Forum.

There were a few after-effects from the suspension. At the time the suspension was handed down, the Rocket, who had never won a scoring championship, was leading the league. While he was sitting out, his teammate Boom Boom Geoffrion passed him to take the title. On the night he scored the goal that put him ahead of the Rocket, Geoffrion was booed by the fans at the Forum, who never quite forgave him for snatching this prize from their hero.

Chapter 2

The Canadiens also lost the Stanley Cup, in a seven-game final to the Detroit Red Wings. There are few, if any, who were in Montreal that spring who aren't convinced it would have been a different story if the Rocket had been allowed to play.

Toe Blake was a teammate of the Rocket on a line with Elmer Lach and later coached the team to five straight Stanley Cups. "I'm sure we would have won a sixth if the Rocket hadn't retired," he said. "There [were] none like him when it came to heart and courage. Maybe there were more rounded players but inside the blue line he was the best."

Most of the Rocket's records, including the 50 goals in 50 games he scored in the 1944–45 season, have long since been eclipsed. His last remaining four records have all been tied by other players. It is remarkable, however, that one of these records stood for many years until tied by Joe Sakic in 2004 and still remains unsurpassed. Rocket achieved this record by scoring six overtime goals in Stanley Cup play. "If you needed a goal to win a big one," Blake once said, "the Rocket was the surest bet to get it."

One year the Montreal Canadiens and Boston Bruins were locked in a game that was going into the second overtime period. Frank Selke, the Canadiens' managing director, was interviewed on television just before the teams returned to the ice.

He was asked who he thought would score the goal that would break up the game. "Rocket Richard," he replied.

What a Riot

The period was less than a minute old when the Rocket blasted one into the net to win it. You couldn't go wrong picking Richard to score in overtime.

Richard's record of 18 game-winning goals in Stanley Cup play has been eclipsed by Wayne Gretzky (24), the greatest player in his era as Rocket was in his, and by Brett Hull (23) and Claude Lemieux (19). Of course, the Stanley Cup playoffs are now much longer than they were in the Rocket's era, when the Canadiens only had to win a maximum of eight games in two series. Now after eight games they are just getting warmed up.

Red Storey refereed hundreds of games in which the Rocket played. "If they're playing hockey a thousand years from now," Storey once said, "there'll never be another Rocket. I've played every game, 'reffed' a thousand more, seen a lot of dedicated men. I never saw one like him, never saw one who was born to do one thing the way he was.

"We're all put on this world for a reason. I've gotta think that when God sent the Rocket he was thinking of hockey."

The Rocket was so upset at his suspension that he told Elmer Ferguson, a veteran columnist for the *Montreal Star*, that he might quit the game. Of course, he didn't. This was man who came alive on a hockey rink as few ever have.

Chapter 2

The game I'll always remember was played in the Montreal Forum in the winter of 1958. The Rocket had broken his leg earlier that season in Toronto and there was speculation his career was over. I went to Montreal not knowing what to expect. Would it be a story of the last hurrah for this great warrior?

The game wasn't two minutes old when I got the answer. Richard took a pass and roared in towards the net, that fire in his eyes that struck fear into the heart of every goaltender who ever played against him. He drilled a shot behind Harry Lumley in the Boston goal. He did it again in the second period and could have had three more goals except Lumley robbed him with big saves.

The Rocket was to play two more seasons on Stanley Cup winners. He says it was his pride that convinced him it was time to retire. "When my gifts [are] gone," he said, "I don't want to hang on being pitied. I wouldn't let that happen."

The Rocket, like Ted Williams, knew when to quit. Williams hit a home run in his last appearance at the plate. The Rocket scored his 626th and final goal on the night of April 12, 1960, in a Stanley Cup final against the Toronto Maple Leafs.

"The last one is a goal I'll never forget," Richard said, "because you know there'll never be another."

I'm often asked which was the greatest hockey team I've ever seen. I'm tempted to make a case for the Edmonton Oilers, who won five Cups, or the New York Islanders, who won four. The Montreal Canadiens in the 1970s deserve an argument, with Guy Lafleur, the most exciting player of his era, Bob Gainey, Larry Robinson, and goalie Ken Dryden. But my vote goes to the Canadiens teams of the 1950s, largely because of the Rocket. Those teams won five in a row and completely dominated the game.

The Canadiens power play with the Rocket and Boom Boom Geoffrion was unstoppable. Under an earlier rule a player could not come out of the box until the full two minutes of a penalty was up. To try to foil the great power play of the Canadiens, the rule was changed, allowing the penalized player to return to the ice if a power play goal was scored. The new rule could not stop the Canadiens when they won their fifth Cup, outscoring the Leafs 15-5 in the Stanley Cup final.

That series was to be the last of the great Rocket Richard. He reported to training camp in the fall, but after scoring four goals in a scrimmage he retired from the game. Only the Rocket would go out like that.

I've often been asked by young colleagues what modern player is the most like Richard. I'm stuck for an answer. Mike Bossy had that same touch around the net but lacked the fire. The Rocket was in a class by himself. He's one of a handful of athletes who you couldn't take your eyes off when he was on the ice. You never knew what you might miss.

The Rocket had to be something special. He's the only hockey player who was suspended and set off a riot.

3

They Did Have Glory Years:
The Toronto Argos

AS LONG AS I can remember, the Argos were the football team I either loved or hated. In between, they've broken both my heart and my wallet, driven me to despair, and provided some of the great moments in a lifetime devoted to avoiding holding down a steady job.

Oh, how we hated the Argos in Sarnia, the western Ontario city where I was born and spent the first 18 years of my life. I was too young to go to the 1933 Grey Cup game played in Sarnia between the Argos and the hometown Imperials, champions of the Ontario Rugby Football Union (ORFU). The Grey Cup is now awarded to the best team in the CFL, but they used to have interleague play back then with the college teams. Both Varsity and Queens have won the Grey Cup.

Chapter 3

The CFL record book shows the Argos won the game 4-3 but no one in Sarnia believed it. Oldtimers in the city will tell you they saw the spot on the sidelines where an official ruled Norm Perry had gone out of bounds on his way to what would have been the winning touchdown. Perry, who later became mayor of Sarnia, didn't go out of bounds, and the cleat marks, or so they tell me, clearly proved it. Everyone knew it except Jo-Jo Stirrett, a Sarnia native, who ruled he went out of bounds at the 42-yard line.

This bit of "treachery" may explain the lifelong antipathy I've had for football officials. It denied Sarnia a Grey Cup that should have been theirs.

It took a long time to get over the feeling that the Argos represented everything bad about Toronto, the city the rest of Canada felt would do us all a favour if it would just disappear into Lake Ontario. When I moved to Toronto in 1948 for a job with the *Toronto Star*, nothing changed my opinion.

The 1952 Grey Cup game between the Argos and the Edmonton Eskimos was the first I covered. I was assigned to cover the Eskimos dressing room, certain that's where the champagne corks would be popping. The Argos won the game and I'd let my prejudice against them get in the way of good judgement. It was certainly not the first, or last time, I was to do it, and I have the empty wallet to prove it.

How could you go against a team that up to then had never lost a Grey Cup to a team from the west? The "lucky old Argos" won it on a pass from Nobby Wirkowski to Zeke

O'Conner, the fifth Grey Cup for the double blue since the end of World War II. None of us suspected it'd be 31 years before they won another.

It could be just a coincidence, but the Argos were Grey Cup champions in 1952 just before I replaced Annis Stukus, who had gone west to coach the B.C. Lions, as the football writer for the *Toronto Star*. I covered the team for eight years but they never really got close to drinking champagne from the Cup.

As long as they were winning, the Argos were easy to hate. But how could you stay mad at a team that struggled from one disaster to another as they did in the 1950s and '60s, changing from the most disliked team in Canada to loveable losers.

You name it, the Argos did it in the almost 20 years they spent in the wilderness. They also provided some of the more unforgettable moments in this sportswriter's career.

I've written a lot of things that annoyed people. I've been threatened, but only once have the words turned into action.

Bob Shaw, who had once scored five touchdowns in an NFL game for the Chicago Cardinals and had never quite gotten over it, was at the tail end of his career when he joined the Argos for the 1954 season. He had played for Calgary before heading to the East. Shaw was a fine pass receiver but his blocking left a lot to be desired.

Chapter 3

I wrote a story about Shaw for the *Star* that was not exactly complimentary. "When Shaw played in Calgary," I wrote, "the mayor said he'd declare a civic holiday every time he threw a block. In three years with the Stampeders no one got as much as 15 minutes off work."

Shaw was not amused and I don't blame him. It was the sort of smart aleck thing that brash young sportswriters come up with. That night when I got to the Argo practice I was told "Shaw's looking for you."

The team used to eat at a restaurant across the road from Varsity Stadium where they played. I'd always made it a point to show up the day after I've written something that was controversial. That night discretion might have been the better part of valour but I was young and foolish.

As soon as I walked in the door, Shaw got up and charged at me. He swung at me but I ducked and the blow glanced off my shoulder. Fortunately, some of his teammates, who weren't exactly enamored of the "big lazy end," grabbed him. I guess the only fight I've had in this business would go into the books as a "no decision." It's just as well because I gave away at least 50 pounds and a couple of inches to Shaw.

It wasn't easy to turn a Grey Cup team into a national joke but the Argos worked at it. Harry Sonshine had played for the Argos in the 1930s. His chief claim to fame is that he was one of the last in the league to play without a helmet. This could have something to do with the way he acted in the two tumultuous years he ran the Argos. Shortly after he was appointed, Sonshine called the football writers to a meeting at his posh apartment in midtown Toronto. After a couple of drinks, he announced he was firing all of the eight imports from the previous year's team and replacing them with NFL stars. One of the players who got the chop was Dick Shatto, then a rookie. He had been the quarterback at the University of Kentucky under Bear Bryant, a legendary US college football coach who turned Shatto into a halfback, and a great one.

When the league stepped in and allowed Sonshine only four of his NFL stars, he had to back down. He hired back Shatto, who went on to become the all-time Argo leader in several offensive categories.

Sonshine also got rid of Frank Clair, who had coached the Argos to the last two Grey Cups they'd won. Clair went to Ottawa where he was to win three more national championships.

In the Sonshine years we used to claim the Argos had three teams. There was the one on the field, and the two at the airport. One was leaving town, the other arriving.

Out went Sonshine, in came a new set of owners headed by John Bassett, the publisher of the *Toronto Telegram*. They brought back Lew Hayman, the team's coach in the 1930s, as managing director.

Chapter 3

Hayman signed Ronnie Knox to play quarterback and at long last it appeared the Argos were on their way back to respectability. I've watched a lot of fine quarterbacks in both the CFL and NFL but I don't believe any of them can throw the football with a better touch than Knox had. He joined the team midway through the 1958 season but by then Argos were out of the playoff picture. Argo fans could hardly wait for the next year, when the team would leave Varsity for the CNE Stadium, where there were another 10,000 seats. With Knox at quarterback, the Argos were sure they would have no trouble filling them.

Knox fancied himself a poet. The *Telegram*, Bassett's paper, ran one of his poems on the front page and Knox was never quite the same—he seemed more interested in his poetry than football. Hamp Pool, then the Argo coach, came from the Los Angeles Rams where he had a good career. He died in May of 2000, and I'm sure he went to his grave wondering what Ronny Knox was up to.

The *Star* struck back by hiring Knox to write a column after every game. The poet wasn't much for prose. He hired me as his ghost. I used to meet with him the day after the game to get his thoughts for the column. One Sunday after we had finished, Knox tossed this bombshell at me.

"I'm quitting the Argos," he said.

"At the end of the season?" I asked.

"I've played my last game," he replied. "I'll be out of here tomorrow."

Asked what he was going to do, Knox replied, "I'm going to write poetry." As a parting shot he said that football was a "game for animals."

I used the quote in the story I wrote to break the news that the world had lost a quarterback and gained a poet. It's a quote that keeps appearing in stories about the violence of football.

Knox originally planned to sneak out of town, booking passage with the travel agency owned by Hamp Pool, the coach of the team. I convinced him he should at least meet with Hayman, the man who had hired him.

Hayman tried his best to talk Knox out of his decision but the quarterback had made up his mind. He never played another game of football, though the Chicago Bears, who held his NFL rights, offered him a big contract if he'd join them. The last I heard Knox was selling real estate in California, but where he is now I have no idea. He had long since decided poetry was not his calling. He remains one of the more unforgettable characters I've ever met, the only quarterback I've ever heard of who turned in his shoulder pads for a poet's pen. It could only happen to the Argos.

The next quarterback to appear on the scene was Tobin Rote, who in 1957 had quarterbacked the Detroit Lions to the NFL championship. Bassett was determined to make a favourable impression when the quarterback flew in for contract talks. The owner wore a coonskin coat when he went to the airport in his chauffeur-driven Bentley to meet Rote. As he walked through the airport, Rote took one look at the owner and muttered, "I thought I was coming up here to play pro football not quarterback Princeton."

The Argos did sign Rote for $30,000 a season, which is peanuts by today's standards. But in 1960 it was more money than all but a handful of NFL quarterbacks were earning. Rote turned out to be a bargain. He quarterbacked the Argos to first place and filled the stadium for all of their home games.

Rote had been a teammate of the legendary Bobby Layne with the Detroit Lions. They were the party team of the NFL, a tradition that Rote brought with him to the Argos.

One night early in the 1960 season, Rote left a party to come to a game against the Montreal Alouettes. He was feeling no pain but it didn't seem to have any effect on his performance. That night Tobin shredded the Alouettes defence, completing 38 passes—at the time a record for pro football. Rote admitted he'd been drinking the afternoon of the game when reporters questioned him afterwards. There was little point in denying it. The smell of stale beer on his breath was a dead giveaway.

Rote had a solid supporting cast that included Chester Carlton (Cookie) Gilchrist who may well have been the most talented athlete ever to play in the CFL. Cookie was as close to a one-man gang as I've ever seen. He was a fullback by trade. But he also played at linebacker, and filled in at defensive tackle, and didn't look out of place at either, for a playoff game with Ottawa.

I have another reason for remembering Cookie. He's the only athlete who ever successfully sued me for libel. In an original story, I mistakenly quoted Eaton Howitt, a writer for the *Hamilton Spectator*, who told me he had seen more of Cookie in court than he did on the football field. Cookie had mishaps with the law, including being taken off the team bus by police for parking tickets that he had not paid. But he had never been charged with any crimes. Gilchrist collected $5,000 in an out-of-court settlement from the *Toronto Star*.

A couple of days after he got the cheque, Cookie showed up at the *Star* office. He wanted me to do him a favour. He was in the electric light business and wondered if I could introduce him to the purchasing agent for the *Star*. I did my best to explain to Cookie that newspapers didn't enjoy being sued. I told him he'd be better off taking his five grand and forgetting about the *Star* as a client.

I've always felt the 1960 Argos were the most talented team of their time. They had a backfield that, in addition to Rote and Cookie, included Dick Shatto and Dave Mann. They toyed with their opposition during the regular season and it seemed the playoffs were just a necessary nuisance. The

Chapter 3

Argos were a sure bet to represent the East in the Grey Cup being played that year in Vancouver.

The East had a two-game total point series back then, in which each team played one game at home and one on the road, with the total points determining the winner. The Argos won the first game in Ottawa and at halftime of the return match at the CNE had a comfortable 12-point lead.

I didn't need to go into the clippings in the *Sun* library to get the details of the Argos collapse. I can remember it as if it happened yesterday. An Ottawa defensive back by the name of Jim Reynolds goofed on his coverage. The man he was supposed to cover was wide open. Reynolds just happened to be there to grab a pass from Rote intended for Shatto. He ran it back for a touchdown. Then Ottawa caught the napping Argos with the hoariest play in the book, a sleeper to Bobby Simpson that worked for another touchdown.

Ottawa headed west to beat Edmonton in one of the more forgettable Grey Cups. The only thing I remember about the game is Angelo Mosca throwing me in the showers when I walked into the Ottawa dressing room. He objected to a story I wrote that the wrong team was representing the East. It cost me a cashmere overcoat that was never quite the same after the dousing.

The '60 Argos collapse was merely a tune-up for the next season. The Argos took an 18-point lead into Hamilton. There was no scoring in the first half of the game so the Argos had 18 points and only 30 minutes to blow it.

They Did Have Glory Years

They managed it in a way you had to see to believe. I did, and over 40 years later I still find it hard to accept. The Tiger-Cats tied up the series and were driving for another score when Stan Wallace intercepted a Bernie Faloney pass and ran it to the Hamilton 25. All the Argos had to do was let Dave Mann, the best punter in the league, put the ball into orbit and the Argos were on their way to the Grey Cup.

It wasn't easy to blow this one but the Argos managed. They tried to pull Hamilton offside but wound up being called themselves and sent back five yards. A draw play lost them five more. When it came time for Mann to kick, Faloney was able to run it out of the end zone and Hamilton went on to win in overtime.

It was to be 10 years before the Argos were to get to a Grey Cup, with Joe Theismann as quarterback and Leo Cahill as the talking man's football coach.

No one could ever deny Leo had a way with words. He took his Argos into Ottawa for the 1969 eastern final, vowing it would "take an act of God" to beat them. We knew they were in trouble when Russ Jackson was spotted walking to the park on the waters of the Rideau Canal. Of course, we were being facetious—even Jackson couldn't walk on water, but sometimes you thought he could.

On one occasion, Commissioner Jake Gaudaur suspended Ed Harrington, an Argo lineman, for one game for rough play. After the game that Harrington sat out, Cahill had the entire team line up on the field and presented the game ball to the suspended player. Commissioner Gaudaur was not amused, but he let Cahill get away with it.

Tom Wilkinson quarterbacked the Argos that season. But owner Bassett didn't think the pudgy little guy fit the image of an Argo quarterback. He was shipped west where as a quarterback of the Edmonton Eskimos he was to win a Schenley Award as the outstanding player in Canada. He joined Peter Liske in Calgary and Don Jonas in Winnipeg as quarterbacks the Argos got rid of who went on to win the top player award.

Bassett told Cahill to find a new quarterback and money was no object. Leo wound up with Theismann, who made a pit stop in Toronto on his way to the NFL, where he was to quarterback the Washington Redskins to a Super Bowl.

In 1971, the Argos were once again "the best team money could buy." This time they managed to get past Hamilton in the eastern final and headed to Vancouver for a Grey Cup game they were favoured to win.

Perhaps it was an omen. One of their players, Joe Vijuk, missed the plane taking the Argos to Vancouver. The Argos checked into a hotel across the street from a strip joint. I wouldn't say it was noisy but one of the patrons was shot dead. No one noticed until he left his three beers sitting on the table. It was not like the dear departed to miss a round.

They Did Have Glory Years

You just knew something bad was going to happen to the Argos. Leon McQuay, a mercurial running back, was the next victim of the Argo jinx. McQuay fumbled on the five yard line in the final minute of a game; the Argos lost by three points. Harry Abofs compounded the felony by booting a punt out of bounds to deny his team one more chance with the football.

The Argos were finally to win a Grey Cup in 1983 in Vancouver. The winning touchdown was scored by Cedric Minter. But football fans who'll never forget McQuay and his fumble are hard pressed to remember the hero of their first win in more than 30 years.

During the postwar years, the team's owners were the directors of the old Argonaut Rowing Club, true Canadians who seldom appeared in public without their blue blazers and Argo crests. I'm sure they were spinning in their graves when Harry Ornest sold the team to Bruce McNall, the owner of the Los Angeles Kings. The team that won three Grey Cups after the war with an all-Canadian lineup was now owned by an American.

McNall signed Rocket Ismail to a $20-million-plus contract, which would make him the highest paid player in all of football, including the NFL. It was the Rocket who ran back a punt 87 yards for the winning touchdown in the Grey Cup game in Winnipeg.

Chapter 3

The Argos had come full circle, from the penthouse to the outhouse and back to the top again. Love 'em or hate 'em, and in my lifetime I've done both, you have to admit there's no team in Canadian sport quite like the Argos. They may drive you up the wall, but at least they're interesting. After all, this is the team that won the 2004 Grey Cup the year after they went bankrupt. But that's the way it has always been for this franchise.

4

Grand National Drunk:
The Grey Cup

ALL I CAN SAY TO the high rollers who want to bring the National Football League to Canada is a pox on all your houses.

There are a lot of reasons I hope I don't live long enough to see the "real football," as its supporters call it ad nauseam, move north of the 49th parallel. But the biggest one, in my view, is that it would mean the end of the Grey Cup, my all-time favourite sporting event. If we were to trade the Grey Cup for the Super Bowl we would wind up with the ultimate in all-American hype. The Super Bowl is indeed a sporting event that has sold its soul to corporate America. One thing you have trouble finding at a Super Bowl are real football fans, the kind that have been having fun, and making fools of themselves, at Grey Cups for more than 80 years.

Chapter 4

The "Grand National Drunk," as the late Dick Beddoes used to call the Grey Cup when he was writing a sports column for *The Globe and Mail*, is still the biggest blast we have in this country. If there is one nation on the face of the earth that deserves a party in the last week of November, surely the dreariest month of the 12, it is Canada.

I've been hooked on the Grey Cup for as long as I can remember. Since 1949, I've been to 50 consecutive Grey Cup games. As mentioned earlier, I grew up in Sarnia, and it was hard not to get the football bug growing up in that western Ontario city, then with a population of 18,000. It was the dirty '30s when finding a job in the midst of the Great Depression was impossible for millions of Canadians and Americans, unless you happened to be a football player.

Orm Beach, an all-American from Kansas, was one of the most talented players ever to come to Canada. He played fullback, backed up the line, and in his spare time kicked field goals. He came north for a job in the Imperial Oil refinery. Beach was the kingpin of a Sarnia team that won the Grey Cup in 1934 and repeated it two years later. Sarnia hasn't competed for the Grey Cup for more than 60 years but they've still won the same number as the Saskatchewan Roughriders.

The first bet I ever made was on a Grey Cup game. I wagered 25 cents, then the price of a haircut, with a barber that Winnipeg would beat Hamilton in the 1935 game. The Bombers won on the magical feet of Fritzie Hanson, the first time the trophy ever went west.

I finally got to see my first Grey Cup game in 1942. I'd come to Toronto with a high school buddy. We were both staying with relatives in Toronto, so we agreed to meet on the morning of the game in Eaton's toy town. It was December 5, less than three weeks before Christmas. The two small town boys couldn't have picked a worse place to meet. We never did find each other in the crowd, which was a problem since my buddy had the tickets.

I went up to Varsity Stadium where getting a ticket was a cinch. I bought a seat on the 40-yard line for $2.50. I was walking away from the wicket when my buddy showed up. I had a tough time talking the ticket seller into giving me my money back. It wasn't too many years before the Grey Cup ticket became the toughest in town (tickets for last year's game in Ottawa started at $120 for endzone seats), a situation that was to continue in Toronto 'til the 1992 game, when they couldn't sell out SkyDome for the game between Winnipeg and Calgary.

The RCAF Hurricanes, coached by Lew Hayman, who had masterminded the Argos to three Grey Cups before the war, beat Winnipeg 8-5 on that cold and blustery afternoon in 1942. The players on both teams were soon headed overseas for a much deadlier game, one from which some of them would not return.

Chapter 4

The Grey Cup was just a football game 'til 1948. That year, the Calgary Stampeders came east and their supporters stood old Toronto on its ear. They brought their horses into the lobby of the Royal York Hotel and convinced Hiram (Buck) McCallum, the mayor of Toronto, to don a cowboy suit and ride a horse up Bay Street. The Stampeders beat Ottawa 12-7, with the winning touchdown scoring on a sleeper play that caught the favoured eastern team napping. The Grey Cup was never to be the same again.

Over the years I attended 50 consecutive Grey Cups. They haven't all been happy experiences. I bet $50, a week's salary in 1950, on Winnipeg to beat the Argos. This was the infamous Mud Bowl at Varsity Stadium when referee Hec Crichton turned over Buddy Tinsley, a Winnipeg lineman who was face down in the goo, and probably saved him from drowning. It was one of the more miserable afternoons of my life. I got soaked as I sat there watching both my money and the Bombers disappear in the mud.

Football is a sport that seems to attract characters. One of them was George Trafton, who had played with the Chicago Bears as a big, tough centre in the early years of the National Football League. He came north in 1953 to coach Winnipeg and I've never met a coach like him before or since. Trafton spent most of the season feuding with his quarterback, Indian Jack Jacobs, one of those larger-than-life figures who then played out west. There was no television of the western games so the fans had to rely on newspaper reports. I was one of the reporters who used to cover the western playoffs and admit to indulging in a bit of purple prose when recording the exploits of Indian Jack.

Jacobs, who had played in the NFL with the Green Bay Packers, felt he knew more about football than his coach. So, he refused to run the plays that Trafton sent in from the bench and called his own. The coach came up with an ingenious idea to foil his quarterback. He used his backup quarterback Joe Zaleski in the backfield and had him call the plays, which Jacobs would then execute. Trafton underestimated Jacobs. Zaleski would call one play, Jacobs would run another, and somehow, in spite of it, the Bombers beat a good Edmonton team in the western final and headed to Toronto for the Grey Cup.

Trafton was convinced his assistant coaches were undermining him, so he fired them the week before the Grey Cup. He recruited Les Lear, who had coached Calgary to the 1948 championship and who was then, as they say, between engagements. Lear and Trafton showed up in Montreal to scout the Alouettes and Hamilton in the eastern final. They got into an argument on the roof of Delormier Downs, the old baseball park where the Als played in their early years. Words turned into punches and it was fortunate they both didn't fall off the roof onto the field.

Those were wild and crazy guys. Hamilton beat the Alouettes, and that night in the lobby of the Mount Royal

Hotel, Jimmie Simpson was running up and down the lobby shouting, "We won, we won."

Simpson, who had played with Hamilton when they lost the 1935 game to Winnipeg, had been the referee that afternoon. At least Jimmie, unlike some other officials at the time, made no secret of his bias. When he hung up his whistle he became the trainer of the Tiger-Cats.

The Schenley Awards started in 1953 at the Granite Club, a hangout of the Toronto establishment. They had an open bar, and by the time they got around to presenting the trophy to Billy Vessels of the Edmonton Eskimos, the guests were in a happy mood. The president of Schenley's and two of the trustees missed the handoff. They fell off the stage with the trophy as Vessels stood there waiting to accept it.

At least Vessels got in the front door of the exclusive Toronto club. Rollie Miles, an Edmonton teammate, was nominated in 1954 and had to be snuck in by a side door. Miles was black and the only ones of his colour on the premises were waiters and kitchen help.

The Tiger-Cats won the '53 Grey Cup 12-6 when a Jacobs pass to Tom Casey was batted away on the goal line in the last play of the game. The result should not have been a surprise to the readers of the *Toronto Star*. Earlier that year the paper, where I was then employed, sent me to Richmond,

Virginia to interview Lady Wonder, a "talking" horse. (Papers did these sorts of things 40 years ago.) Actually, the horse didn't talk, but gave her answers by hitting her nose on the keyboard of a giant typewriter. I know it sounds ridiculous, but since Lady Wonder and the lady who owned her are both dead, you'll have to take my word for it. The *Star* ran the story, with a picture of their reporter interviewing the horse, on the front page. Among other predictions, the horse picked Hamilton to win the Grey Cup.

My wife was at Varsity Stadium for a game in the '53 season as Hamilton was giving the Argos a good old-fashioned whipping. A fan sitting nearby was yelling at the Argos for their lousy play. "Don't get upset, Dad," the leather-lunged fan's son said. "The horse said Hamilton was going to win the Grey Cup."

Jim Kingsbury, the *Star*'s managing editor, suggested I go back to interview the horse the next year. I talked him out of it. I felt both Lady Wonder and I should quit while we were still ahead.

I doubt if either Lady Wonder or I would have been able to predict the result of the 1954 Grey Cup, one of the greatest upsets in the history of the game. The late Bob Frewin, writing in the *Toronto Telegram*, described the Eskimos as a "two buck team in a quarter million dollar spectacle." It enraged the Eskimos but there were only a few, outside of Edmonton, who felt they had a chance against one of the most explosive teams in the history of Canadian football.

With an offence that featured quarterback Sam Etcheverry throwing to Red O'Quinn and Harold Patterson, plus Alex Webster, later to star in the NFL with the New York Giants, running the ball, the Als were expected to easily justify the 18-point spread.

Roy Robertson, a Montreal stockbroker who owned the Alouettes, must have thought so. He wagered $100,000 on his team and when they lost, 26-25, had to sell the team to pay off the bet.

One of the big winners was Bob Kashower, an Edmonton motel owner. He was so grateful to the Eskimos that he chartered a plane and flew the team to Montreal for a party. In the 1950s, Toronto's early closing laws were not in tune with the all-night party the Eskimos wanted to celebrate their first Grey Cup.

I've always felt the 1950s was the golden age of Canadian football. One of the reasons was the three Grey Cups between Edmonton and Montreal.

Another highlight of the '50s was the hosting of the 1955 game by Vancouver, the first time it had been played in the west. It was one of the best things that ever happened to the Grey Cup; it was becoming a truly national sports event. It helped that the two teams put on a dazzling display of football. Etcheverry passed for more than 500 yards but the Eskimos wore Montreal down with their powerful running game featuring their twin fullbacks, Johnny Bright and Normie Kwong. Jackie Parker not only quarterbacked the

In 1949, I was arrested while covering a strike at Penmans textile factory for the *Toronto Star* in Paris, Ontario. The police thought I was one of the strikers and dragged me off, but the Star explained everything and got me out of there. Anyway, Norm James took me out to the parking lot to get this picture, under orders from the publisher to make me look like a young Lindbergh. (Photo by Norm James, courtesy of Jim Hunt.)

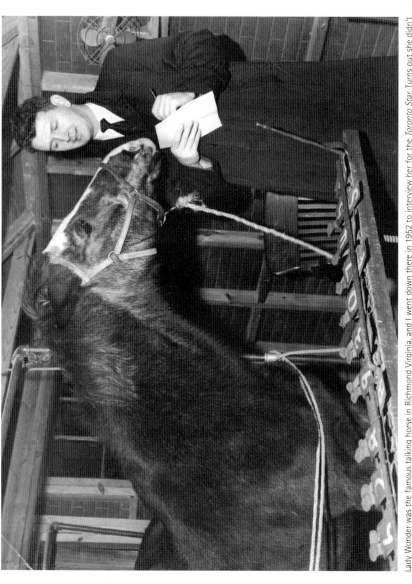

Lady Wonder was the famous talking horse in Richmond Virginia, and I went down there in 1952 to interview her for the *Toronto Star*. Turns out she didn't really talk; she hit a sort of typewriter with her nose to spell out words. I asked her who would win the 1953 Grey Cup and she correctly predicted that Hamilton would take it. (Photo courtesy of Jim Hunt.)

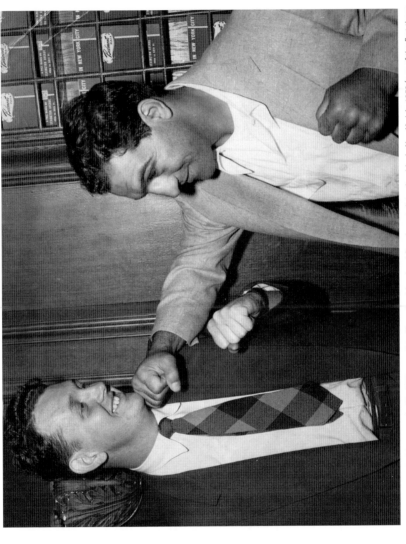

Rocky Marciano had just won the World Heavyweight Championship when I flew down to interview him in New York in 1953 (one of the first times I was ever on an airplane). He'd knocked out Jersey Joe Walcott to win the title and went on to retire as the only undefeated champion in boxing history. (Photo by Eric Cole, courtesy of Jim Hunt.)

In 1956, there was a security problem at Maple Leaf Gardens and the *Star* had the bright idea of having me walk in with a gun, which I did without being stopped. The "gun" was a wooden mock-up and this photo ran on the front page of the *Star* the next day. (Photo by Paul Smith, courtesy of Jim Hunt.)

Joe Kapp, on the right, was the quarterback for the BC Lions when this photo was taken in the early 1960s. He led the Lions to the Grey Cup in 1964, and went on to play in the Super Bowl with the Minnesota Vikings. He was one of the more colourful players in the CFL. (Photo courtesy of Jim Hunt.)

Maury Wills was the first to break Ty Cobbs' base-stealing record in 1962 with 104 steals when he was playing for the LA Dodgers. (Photo courtesy of Jim Hunt.)

British racecar driver Stirling Moss sits behind the wheel in this photo taken in the early 1960s at Mosport Park north of Bowmanville, Ontario. On press day before the Canadian Grand Prix, he invited newspapermen to go around the track with him. I took him up on his offer and he scared the hell out of me. When he realized I was getting scared, he went faster. Stirling was one of the world's great drivers though, and I was probably safer with him than driving with a neighbour on Highway 401. But I wasn't nervous, really. (Photo courtesy of Jim Hunt.)

Stan Musial of the St. Louis Cardinals was of course one of the all-time great baseball players when this photo was taken in the early 1960s. (Photo courtesy of Jim Hunt.)

Eskimos but played safety on defence. It was an iron man act no Grey Cup quarterback has even attempted since.

The two teams went at it the next year in Toronto. This time Parker switched to halfback and Don Getty, later to be premier of Alberta, quarterbacked the Eskimos. Parker scored three touchdowns and Getty two as the Eskimos rolled to a 50-27 win. It was the game where they ran out of footballs. As a result, the Eskimos never did get around to kicking the convert on the final touchdown. That point cost at least one Montreal fan the $5,000 he would have won in a pool if Edmonton had made the convert, which was almost automatic.

When he got back to his hotel room, the fan who had missed winning the pool by a single point was greeted by his teenage son who had sat in the end zone.

"Look, Dad," was his greeting. "I got one of the balls they kicked into the stands." His father didn't seem too impressed with his son's Grey Cup souvenir.

This was to be the last Montreal–Edmonton game for at least a few years. It was time for a new cast to take over centre stage. The Hamilton Tiger-Cats and Winnipeg Blue Bombers were to play six times in nine years, and all of them were games worth remembering.

Jim Trimble, a bombastic man who was in love with his own voice, coached the Tiger-Cats. Bud Grant, who had played for Trimble when he coached the Philadelphia Eagles, was now coaching the Bombers. Trimble won the first meeting between the master and his pupil. The Tiger-Cats rolled 32-7 over a Winnipeg team, battered from a tough western final that ended the Edmonton dynasty, but it's a game that's remembered for an incident that became a part of Grey Cup lore.

Bibbles Bawel, a defensive back for the Tiger-Cats, intercepted a Winnipeg pass and headed for the end zone. As he raced down the sidelines, a spectator, standing on the sideline, tripped him with his foot. The tripper disappeared into the crowd. It wasn't 'til much later it was revealed he was Dave Humphrey, a young trial lawyer who was later to be a judge. He had cadged the sideline pass from Doug Creighton, a police reporter for the *Toronto Telegram*. The latter too went on to bigger and better things as one of the founders of the *Toronto Sun*.

The lawyer showed a touch of class. That Christmas, Bawel received a watch. On the back was engraved, "From the Grey Cup Tripper."

The 1958 game was played in Empire stadium in Vancouver and Trimble set the tone by boasting "we'll waffle them" as he took his team west.

It's one Grey Cup I'll never forget, not so much because of the game, which was one of the best I've seen, but the trouble I got in from a story that appeared on the front page of the *Toronto Star*.

I was in the Arctic Club, a popular Vancouver night spot in the 1950s, the Thursday before the game. To my surprise a dozen members of the Tiger-Cats walked in. When the bar closed, we adjourned to an after hours club where the booze flowed 'til dawn.

I wrote what I thought was a humorous piece about the Tiger-Cats being so cocky they partied till dawn while the Bombers were in their beds by the 11 p.m. curfew. The headline writer didn't help my cause when he came up with this gem: "Cocky Tiger-Cats party till dawn."

The next day I was called by Jake Gaudaur, then the president of the Tiger-Cats. He wanted to meet me in his hotel suite and I had an idea this wasn't just a social call. When I arrived, Trimble was standing at door and I knew I was in for it. I've seldom seen anyone as mad. I've always felt Gaudaur, who was there with Trimble, saved me from being punched out by his irate coach. Trimble stormed out of the room with this parting shot: "Hunt, I'll never speak to you again."

The Hamilton players threatened to write my wife suggesting I had no business being out 'til 5 a.m. either. I've often wondered if I should have written the story. My only defence was the one I gave Trimble when he asked how I knew the players were out 'til dawn. "I was there, Jim," I told him. I declined to name the players when Trimble asked, because I hadn't used their names in the story.

No one can confuse the Tiger-Cats of leaving their game on the town. The Bombers won 35-28 in what goes down as the best of the 50 Grey Cups I've watched. The loss was a terrible blow to Trimble's ego. It was bad enough to lose but to be beaten by one of his former players was more than Jungle Jim could stand.

The next year the teams met again in the first Cup to be played at Toronto's CNE Stadium. Quarterback Bernie Faloney recalls that Trimble was so desperate to outsmart Grant that he changed his offence twice during the week of the game. On the way to the stadium, Faloney remembers turning to teammate John Barrow and saying, "John, I have no idea what offence we're using. Is it the one we used all season or the one the coach put in this week? He's already changed it a couple of times."

Despite the confusion, which cost them a touchdown when fullback Gerry McDougall went the wrong way at the Winnipeg two yard line, the Tiger-Cats put up a great fight before losing 21-7.

The Bombers won again in 1961 but had to go into overtime to do it. Kenny Ploen, the Bomber quarterback, scampered down the sidelines for the winning touchdown, the one and only Grey Cup where they've needed a fifth quarter to decide it.

The two teams were back again in 1962 and this time it was the weatherman who took over. The Fog Bowl may well have been the best Grey Cup no one saw. It was finally halted with 10 minutes to play when fog engulfed the field. The game was finished Sunday when only 10,000 of the 32,655 fans who had been there Saturday showed up. The ones who stayed home didn't miss much. Neither team scored, so the Bombers held on for a 28-27 win, the only Grey Cup it took two days to decide.

They don't make football players, or sportswriters, like they once did. The late Ted Reeve, who played in a couple of Grey Cups in the 1920s, was one of the last of the breed. He got to the '65 game between Hamilton and Winnipeg and settled down in his seat. There was a 50-mile-an-hour wind blowing from the west and when the Tiger-Cats won the toss and took the ball instead of the wind, Reeve was so upset he just walked out and went home.

5

The Greatest Athlete:
Muhammad Ali

THERE ARE ONLY A handful of people for whom you remember the first time you set eyes upon them—people who could light up a room with the force of their personality.

Cassius Marcellus Clay, still three years and a name change away from the heavyweight championship of the world, was certainly one of the most unforgettable people I've ever met.

It was September 25, 1962, and I was in Chicago to cover the Sonny Liston–Floyd Patterson fight for the heavyweight championship. There wasn't much to remember about the fight, which Liston won with a first round knockout.

The day after the fight, I was having a drink in the press room when Clay, as he was then called, walked in and a crowd of reporters gathered around him. How could you resist this brash, good-looking young man who just two years before had won the gold medal at the Rome Olympics? He was getting ready to fight Archie Moore, who had knocked out his 45th opponent the year Clay had been born.

The man who would change the face of boxing, and in the process become the world's best-known athlete, was known more for his mouth than his skills in the ring. He went into every city where he fought like a candidate for mayor, appearing on television and radio and even going into the beatnik coffee houses to spout poetry.

The poems dealt mostly with what Clay would do to his opponent, including a prediction of in what round he'd win. No one paid too much attention till he fought Moore, still one of the wiliest men ever to lace on a pair of boxing gloves.

"Moore will fall in four," Cassius said. Old Archie went down for the count in the fourth round just as Clay had predicted, and the man who put his fists where his mouth had been became the hottest thing in the heavyweight division.

There was little doubt what Clay had in mind. He was going to become the first man in history to literally talk his way into the heavyweight championship of the world.

After the fight, Clay jumped into the ring where Liston was being crowned as the heavyweight champion. Sonny turned to Clay and said, "You're next, big mouth."

Clay had a tough act to follow the next day in the press room. Norman Mailer had broken up Liston's press conference by challenging the new champion to a fight. The famous author at least had an excuse for this bit of foolishness.

He was drunk and some of his friends pulled him away when he went to challenge Liston.

Cassius waited 'til Mailer had been led away, then he gathered the media around him as he was to do for the rest of his career. At six foot four inches and 200 pounds, I happened to be the biggest in the group. Cassius pointed to me and shouted, "You'll be Liston."

"I'm going to hit him with seven straight jabs," Clay said, whistling punches past my ear. "Seven straight jabs and I got him in a corner and boom, a right cross. If he don't go down I turns and runs," and as he said it Clay disappeared out the door.

The next time I ran into Clay was in a hotel room in New York. He was still talking a great fight but no one took him seriously. He had crashed Liston's victory party in Las Vegas after the champion had knocked out Patterson for a second time.

Liston, in a rare burst of good humour, said, "Come over here and sit on my knee and finish your orange juice."

Earlier Cassius had been spouting his favourite verse: "Liston may be great but he'll fall in eight." Whereupon Sonny replied, "I'll retire if he lasts eight seconds with me."

Liston, who learned to box in Missouri State Prison, where he was serving time for manslaughter, was one of the most frightening men I've ever met. I interviewed him in the snack bar of a golf club in the Catskills prior to the Patterson fight. It was early spring and no one else was in the place.

Chapter 5

"Sonny," I said, being both young and foolish, "they tell me you have one of the greatest left hooks in the history of boxing, but your right hand isn't much."

Liston clenched his right, waved it in front of my nose and said, "How would you like to find out how good my right is?"

I sputtered a "no thanks" and moved on to other matters, such as his weight and birthday.

Clay, as I discovered that afternoon, didn't find Sonny nearly as frightening as the rest of the world did. He had a plan as well as a poem, and I got them both when I visited him in his midtown Manhattan hotel. My original appointment was for noon. When I showed up, the "do not disturb" sign hung on the door.

Rudolph Clay, the fighter's younger brother, invited me into the living room where an empty bottle from a party the night before sat on the table. Cassius didn't drink, but had scotch and bourbon around for his friends.

Rudolph returned to tell me his brother was sleeping but would see me at 5 p.m.

On my second visit, I was again ushered into the living room of the suite, but this time Clay was seated on a couch between two young women. One of the women, who was introduced to me as Sophia Burton ("as in Sophia Loren and Richard Burton" she told me), got up to leave but Clay pulled her back to the couch. "Stay baby," he said. "These writers always put your name in the story."

The Greatest Athlete

The soon-to-be champion gave me a detailed account of how he planned to fight and beat Liston. It was a plan he was to follow to perfection six months later in Miami when he won the championship in one of the big upsets in boxing history.

As he finished his description, Clay was on his feet punching away at an imaginary opponent. Then he turned back to me and burst into another verse: "After I beat Liston I'll be sad, then there'll be no one to make me mad." After he had given me ample time to copy it down, he repeated it a second time, then turned and asked, "Do I look like a fighter?"

I said he looked more like a lover.

He laughed. "Is that right baby?" he asked Miss Burton.

"Cassius, you're the greatest," she replied. Clay beamed and planted a kiss on her lips.

For a moment Clay became serious. "You know, I really don't like to fight," he said. "I's too pretty and I don't want to mark up this handsome face. But I need the money, oh how I need it." Clay then walked into the bedroom of the suite and returned with a magazine with Liston on the cover. "Did you ever see anything so ugly as that big bear?" he said. "That Liston so ugly," Clay continued, "that his wife goes to the gymnasium with him so she won't have to kiss him goodbye." This old vaudeville line was greeted with howls of laughter.

Clay excused himself to change into an open-necked white shirt, dark gray trousers, and black loafers. As we left

Chapter 5

the suite, he asked me if I had $10. He needed the money to tip the parking doorman who had his red Cadillac convertible brought to the door.

Clay, the two girls, and three men climbed in and set off for a party on a yacht anchored in the Hudson River. I walked back to the hotel to transcribe the notes from the most unusual interview I've ever conducted.

Cassius was to earn a hundred million dollars. I never did get my 10 bucks back but it was worth a hundred times that much to sit in on the show he put on that afternoon.

When I returned to Toronto, my editor, Ray Gardner, wondered if I had another bit of poetry as a lead-in for the story. I phoned Cassius and without hesitating, he rattled one off faster than I could write it down.

It wasn't quite up to T.S. Eliot's standards but as doggerel it wasn't too bad.

> Marcellus vanquished Carthage
> Cassius laid Caesar low
> And Clay will flatten Sonny Liston
> With a mighty, measured blow.

Clay put his fists where his mouth had been that February in Miami Beach when Liston became the first fighter in a heavyweight championship fight to surrender his title while sitting on his stool. It may have been one of the great con jobs of all time. Clay acted like a lunatic, completely out of control at the weigh-in the morning of the fight. The fight writers, most of them who had had enough of his act anyway, were convinced Cassius was scared stiff of Liston. The champion shared their view.

It was soon evident during the fight that Clay was just too fast for the plodding Liston. He was hitting him at will while the champion had trouble landing anything on a fighter who moved as fast as Clay did.

Cassius was winning the fight but as he went to his corner after the fourth round he started to shout, "I can't see, my eyes. Cut the gloves off, we're going home."

His trainer, Angelo Dundee, told him, "Forget the bullshit. This is the heavyweight championship of the world and you're winning the fight." Dundee pushed Clay down, rinsed out his eyes with a sponge and pushed him into the ring as the bell sounded. "This is the big one, daddy. Stay away from him, run" were Dundee's parting words to his fighter.

Clay followed his instructions to the letter. By the sixth round his eyes had cleared up and he was able to resume the attack on a tiring Liston.

Sonny had had enough. He stayed on his stool when the bell sounded for the seventh round. He claimed his shoulder was hurt, a pretty sad excuse for surrendering his title.

I couldn't help but recall a conversation with Rocky Marciano on the eve of the Liston–Patterson fight in 1961. "Liston is like most big bullies, if you can stay away and make him miss for a few rounds he'll get frustrated," Rocky

Chapter 5

said. "Once you strip away that feeling of invincibility, he can be had."

The former heavyweight champion set out the blueprint that Clay was to use to pull off the upset. Anyone who had listened and bet on Clay, a 7-1 underdog, would have cleaned up.

If the first fight was bizarre, the return match in 1965 was even more so. The fight was originally scheduled for Boston, but when the word surfaced that the champion had become a Black Muslim, the Commonwealth of Massachusetts wanted no part of it. The promoters finally settled on Lewiston, Maine, a town near the Canadian border where a goodly number of the population still spoke French.

Liston was still the favourite because no one would really believe he could possibly lose again to this young upstart with the big mouth. It was a sentiment shared by the fight writers, especially the old generation who wanted no part of a Muslim. They felt more comfortable with the mobsters that surrounded Liston than the Muslims in Clay's camp

It wasn't until years later, and by this time many of the fight writers had died or retired, that the champion was referred to as Muhammad Ali, the Muslim name he had adopted. Ali felt he had good reason to change his name. His forbearers had worked as slaves on the plantation of Cassius

The Greatest Athlete

Marcellus Clay, Lincoln's ambassador to Russia, and, as was the case with many slaves, they took the name of their master. It is worth remarking that Ambassador Clay became an abolitionist by 1840 and fought against slavery.

Liston was an ex-con but in the eyes of many members of the media, and a good segment of the American public, he was their choice. The only crime Clay had committed was to shoot off his mouth.

The fight was held in the Lewiston arena, which held 5,000 people, a far cry from Yankee Stadium, which had been the site of so many heavyweight championship fights. The big money was now in closed circuit television. Perhaps it's just as well they didn't have 50,000 people at this fiasco. They might have stormed the ring, yelling "fix!"

The night started off on a sour note when Bob Goulet forgot the words while singing "The Star-Spangled Banner." He could be excused since he was a Canadian, though I'm not so sure Goulet would have fared any better with our national anthem.

The fight lasted one minute and 52 seconds. Ali landed only three punches. I was at ringside and never saw the short right hand that sent Sonny tumbling to the canvas. Afterwards, in a moment of fancy, Ali claimed he had learned the punch from Stepin Fetchit, a black comedian who was one of the hangers-on at his camp. The only one who bought the story was *Sports Illustrated*, who had diagrams of the "phantom punch" in the issue that reported the story of the fight.

Chapter 5

The magazine, like most newspapers, still called the champ Cassius Clay.

Instead of going to a neutral corner, Ali stood over his fallen opponent, his fist cocked, screaming, "Get up and fight, you sucker."

Jersey Joe Walcott, the former heavyweight champion, who was the referee, appeared to be in a trance. He should have ordered Ali to a neutral corner and started the count. Walcott tried pushing Muhammad away from the fallen Liston but it wasn't until the champion started to dance away that he got him to a corner and started the count.

Seventeen seconds after landing on the canvas, Liston finally got up. Walcott wiped off his gloves and let the fight resume. Meanwhile, from ringside, Nat Fleischer, the publisher of *Ring Magazine*, was screaming, "It's over. He's out."

Walcott turned his back on the fighters, walked over to Fleischer, listened for a moment, returned to the centre of the ring, and stopped the fight.

The next day I was flying back to Toronto. Willie Reddish, Liston's trainer, was in the seat in front of me. I overheard him say to his companion, "I knew that big bum wasn't going to fight much. He was in terrible shape. But I thought he'd have the decency not to go down the first time he got hit."

Heavyweight champion was a title Ali was to hold until he refused induction into the U.S. Army. "I have no quarrel with the Viet Cong," he said, a sentiment shared by millions of young Americans. He was stripped of his title and literally run out of the country. It was Harold Ballard who gave him a place to fight. It could be that Ballard had no more lofty motive than making some money for Maple Leaf Gardens. It was a move that so incensed Conn Smythe, the man who built the Gardens, that he severed any connection he still had with the organization.

Whatever his motives, Ballard gave Ali a place to fight when his own country had blackballed him. The original opponent was to have been Ernie Terrell, but he withdrew under pressure from the media and politicians.

Arthur Daley, the Pulitzer Prize–winning columnist of the *New York Times*, expressed an opinion that was typical. "This fight should not be patronized either in person or on theatre TV," Daley thundered in his column. "Not a nickel should be contributed to the coffers of Clay, the black Muslims, or the promoter who jammed this down so many unwilling throats."

The media in Toronto were much friendlier to Ali, though Milt Dunnell, the respected sports editor of the *Toronto Star*, always referred to him by his old name of Cassius Clay.

The fight, against Canadian champion George Chuvalo, at Maple Leaf Gardens in 1966 was one-sided from the start. From my seat at ringside, I counted the punches. At one point Ali drilled 22 of them at Chuvalo before he got off one in return. Ali often stood with his arms high and allowed

Chuvalo to pound his body. Out of 15 rounds the Canadian won only one.

Chuvalo, who took more punches than any fighter in history, still makes as much sense as he ever did. It is Ali, who now mumbles so severely he is scarcely comprehensible, who has paid the price for his years in the ring.

The last time I saw Ali was at the Mike Tyson–Frank Bruno fight in Las Vegas in 1989. Tyson, the most brutal champion since Liston, had just knocked out the challenger from England. As his handlers paraded him around the ring to the cheers of the crowd, a middle-aged man was spotted shuffling towards the exit.

It was Ali. I decided to follow him as he plodded along, stopping to shake the hands of admirers along the way.

Ali had once been cheered as few men have been before or since. Now he was just another middle-aged man trying to beat the rush to the exits.

Ali was in Toronto in the fall of 1988 for a dinner to honour Chuvalo. I was invited but declined. I'd like to remember Ali the way he was—the young man who entertained me so long ago in his New York hotel room. The wonderful fighting machine who brought science to a brutal sport.

He was one of a kind and I doubt if I'll ever see his like again.

6

The Greatest Games:
The Canada–Russia Hockey Series

I'M SURE THE EAST YORK Lyndhursts didn't realize what they started when they lost the 1954 World Hockey championships to the Soviets.

"Russians Beat Toronto Used Car Lot" was the headline in the *Montreal Gazette*. The rest of the media, and the country at large, didn't find it nearly as funny. Hockey is our game and we were insulted that the Soviets could beat us, even if the team we sent overseas was not even a first-rate amateur squad. As long as we kept winning, no one paid much attention to the world championships.

When we lost, especially to the Russians, it was a slight to our national honour. We found it hard to accept the fact that anyone could beat us at our game. The Penticton V's did beat the Soviets at the 1955 world championships played in

Chapter 6

West Germany but, as we were soon to realize, this was merely a reprieve for Canadian hockey.

The on-ice rivalry between Canada and the Soviet Union was to become the biggest sports story in my lifetime. It was a battle fought on the ice rinks of the world between two contrasting ways of life. It was brought into focus for this reporter on Easter Sunday in Vienna, Austria, site of the 1967 world championships.

I was sitting in the hotel lobby when first the Canadians, led by their mentor Father David Bauer (hockey player turned priest, and coach of the Canadian team), walked through on their way to church. A few minutes later the Soviets came by dressed in sweatsuits. They were on their way to play soccer in the park across the street. This was part of their training program. That night the Soviet way of life prevailed with a 2-1 win.

We always had one cop-out when the Soviets kept beating us: our best players were in the NHL and it'd be a different story if and when we sent the hockey elite against them.

The stage was set for the most anticipated sports event in Canadian history, the 1972 summit between Canada and the Soviets. I'm sure the NHL never thought for a moment they would lose. Otherwise they wouldn't have agreed to the series. They were so arrogant that Bobby Hull, the best left winger in hockey, was not allowed to play for Team Canada. Hull was being punished for jumping to the World Hockey Association. His absence made it to the floor of the House of

Commons. But the NHL didn't care. They were certain they'd win without the game's greatest left winger.

The series started on September 2, 1972, in the Montreal Forum. Canadian hockey was never going to be the same again.

I was sitting beside Bill Stephenson, the sportscaster for CFRB in Toronto. Team Canada scored two quick goals and I remember turning to my seatmate and saying, "Bill, how are we going to keep this story alive for eight games? It could be over tonight." This has to rate up there with the dumbest things I've ever said. Canada was never in the game after the first 10 minutes and afterwards everyone from NHL president Clarence Campbell on down was trying to find someone to blame.

I flew back to Toronto where the second game was to be played. The kids were playing ball hockey on the street outside my bedroom window. "I'm Kharlamov," one shouted. "You can be Yakushev." Esposito, Mahovlich, and the rest of the Canadian superstars no longer rated with the kids. The adults weren't any kinder to their fallen heroes.

Team Canada evened the series up with a win at Maple Leaf Gardens on September 4th. They tied the Soviets in Winnipeg and were booed off the ice in Vancouver. Phil Esposito was so upset at the way the Canadian fans treated the team he went on TV after the game to blast them.

I'm convinced this was the turning point of the series. Team Canada headed overseas knowing they had an uphill battle if they were going to win a series that just a week before no one thought they could possibly lose.

I wouldn't say the Canadian players were paranoid. But Frank Mahovlich was so positive the Russians were bugging their rooms that he wanted the team to camp out in tents on the outskirts of Moscow and be bussed in for the games.

The players weren't the only ones who didn't know quite what to expect when they arrived in beautiful downtown Moscow. A contingent of 2,700 fans accompanied Team Canada to the Soviet Union, at the time the biggest group of sports fans ever to set foot in the country.

The Soviet officials didn't know what to expect from the "unruly Canadians." They brought in a battalion of soldiers who surrounded the rink just in case things got out of hand. They never did.

One thing anyone who was there will never forget is the way the Canadians sang "O Canada" prior to the start of the first game in Moscow, September 22, 1972. I've heard our national anthem sung all over the world but never with the enthusiasm it got that night.

We also found out in a hurry who was running the country. Leonid Brezhnev, the boss of bosses in the Soviet Union, showed up for the first game of the series. Just prior to the faceoff, there was an announcement in both English and Russian that there would be no smoking permitted in the arena. A few moments later, Brezhnev sat down in the VIP box and lit up a cigarette. There was obviously one law for the general secretary of the Communist Party and another for the common folk.

The CTV network, which was carrying the games back to Canada, had made arrangements with the Soviets to allow for stoppages in play so they could get in their commercials. Brezhnev inquired of an aide why play was being halted. He didn't accept the explanation that it was so the capitalists could get in their commercials. He ordered that there be no more delays. There weren't, and viewers back in Canada missed a goal while the network was carrying a commercial.

Team Canada blew a lead and lost the first game in Moscow 5-4. It was the last one they were to lose, thanks to Paul Henderson, who wasn't even supposed to be on this star-studded team. Henderson and his linemates Ron Ellis and Bobby Clarke were picked as cannon fodder when the team was chosen. They were around to scrimmage with the big guns, but they didn't expect to see much action.

As it turned out, they were the best line Team Canada had. Everyone remembers that Henderson scored the winning goal in the eighth and last game, a shot that was heard around the hockey world. What is overlooked is that he also scored the winner in the sixth and seventh game of the series, too.

Henderson was the great Canadian hero in the eyes of everyone except the man who signed his paycheque, Harold Ballard, the owner of the Toronto Maple Leafs. Ballard stopped off in Moscow on his way to jail for tax evasion. Interviewing him in Moscow, I asked him if he wasn't proud of the way Henderson played. "He can score over here because no one hits him," Ballard said. "He won't score like that back in the NHL."

Ballard may have been ungracious but there was an element of truth in what he said. Henderson left the Leafs and first went to the Toronto Toros of the WHA. After two seasons in Toronto he moved with that team when it was moved to Birmingham, but was never again to capture the magic of those wonderful seven days in Moscow.

His linemate Clarke may have made almost as important a contribution to the Canadian victory. He gave Valery Kharlamov, the speedy Soviet winger, a chop across the ankles with his stick in the sixth game. Kharlamov played in the deciding game of the series but he was obviously feeling the effects of the slash. At the time, the "win at any cost" philosophy in the Canadian camp made Clarke's slash just a part of the game. Looking back, even Don Cherry, that great defender of violence in hockey, would have trouble justifying it.

Henderson was the hero, but the big star for Team Canada, at least in the eyes of the Russian fans, was Phil Esposito, the centre of the Boston Bruins. One night my wife and I went with another couple to a Georgian restaurant in Moscow that offered a break from the steak and french fries they served in the hotel. A Russian came up to my wife obviously wanting to ask her to dance. "Esposito," he said. This was the only English he knew but Caroline got the message.

The Greatest Games

One day I was walking with Brian Williams, the CBC sportscaster, near the United States embassy. We spotted a young man with a Monopoly game under his arm. We were sure we were onto a good story. That ultimate capitalist board game had come to the Soviet Union. I went up to the young man, pointed, and said, "Mon-op-oly." He looked at me as I'd taken leave of my senses. "I'm an American," he said in an accent that was straight out of Brooklyn.

Williams and I teamed up again after the final game and I still don't believe we got away with it. Henderson was being interviewed on television and we were determined we were going to get to talk to him. Two burly Soviet policemen had other ideas. They put up their hands and said nyet, which was no way in Russian.

I handed my tape recorder to Williams and told him to follow me. I went between the two Soviet cops like a defensive end going for the quarterback. Williams followed me in. I still don't know why we weren't arrested as we surely would have been if we had tried to do the same thing in Toronto or Montreal. I guess the Russian policemen just couldn't believe anyone would do what we did. We got away with it, got our interviews with Henderson.

A lot of people back home criticized Alan Eagleson when he gave the finger (out of frustration with the refs) to the booing crowd when he went on the ice during that eighth game. Few of us who were in Moscow joined in putting the knock on the Eagle. He wasn't the only one who blew his cool on a night when a lot of us were struck with a temporary case of insanity.

On the way back to the hotel after that game, I met two young ladies in an underpass. They looked at the decal of the Canadian flag on my tape recorder, smiled, and said, "Congratulations. Your team deserved to win."

Would we have been as gallant towards a Russian if they had won the series? I somehow doubt it.

It's been over 30 years since that first hockey summit. I've been to a World Series, Super Bowls, Grey Cups, and Canada Cups but nothing will ever compare with it. This was truly a once in a lifetime event, an opinion I'm sure any of the 2,700 Canadians who were there will agree with.

The next time I hooked up with the Soviet hockey team was at the 1974 world championships played in Helsinki, Finland. I had been assigned to do a magazine article on Valery Kharlamov, who could skate as fast as any hockey player I'd ever seen.

I had told Ballard that I was going to Finland to talk to the Soviet player. "Tell them I'll pay Kharlamov and Yakushev a million dollars each if they'll play for the Leafs," he said. "You'll get $100,000 if you can sign them."

My interpreter for the interview was a very attractive young lady who was working for a Soviet trade mission in

Helsinki. It wasn't until later I found out her father was a colonel in the KGB, the notorious secret police. It was the first time I'd ever been able to talk to one of the Soviet players without a coach and the KGB agent who accompanied the team in the room. I guess they figured they were safe with the colonel's daughter. I did mention to Kharlamov about the offer from Ballard. He just smiled and said, "I'd love to play in the NHL but I'm afraid it's impossible."

Kharlamov did ask if I could get him a copy of the picture a photographer I'd hired had taken with him and the colonel's daughter. That fall the Soviets came to Canada to play the WHA. I met Kharlamov outside the team's dressing room at Maple Leaf Gardens and handed him an envelope with the photographs. He grabbed it and acted as if he'd never set eyes on me though we'd spent more than an hour talking in Helsinki just four months before.

I've always felt Kharlamov would have been a super superstar in the NHL. It was not to be and he died in an automobile accident on August 27, 1981, long before his time.

The NHL may well have decided after the '72 summit that they'd quit while they were ahead. It opened the door for the upstarts from the WHA to go head to head with the Soviets. This allowed players in the WHA to get the recognition that NHL players received. It gave Bobby Hull the chance he missed in 1972. It also meant that Gordie Howe would be able to play with his two sons, Mark and Marty.

Chapter 6

The Soviets found to their sorrow that though Howe was closing in on 50, he still had the best set of elbows in the business. Boris Mikhailov found out the hard way during one of the games in Moscow. The tough Soviet winger made the mistake of giving young Mark Howe a slash behind the goal. No one really saw what happened next. But there was big Gordie skating away while Mikhailov was lying on the ice with a pained expression on his face.

The Soviets believed hockey was a young man's game. They found it hard to believe a man, whose two sons were also on the team, could play as well as Howe did. They didn't realize that Howe was undoubtedly the most amazing athlete in North America. I was convinced that this series would be Gordie's last hurrah. I got one of his sticks, and had it autographed for my youngest son, Andrew—a great souvenir of Howe's last game. Little did I know this great warrior would be playing another six years before he finally hung up his skates.

I flew with the team from Vancouver, over the pole to Helsinki. The night we arrived a few of us were having a beer in the hotel with Gordie and his wife Colleen. She dozed off. Gordie leaned across the table and said, "Shh, don't wake her up. It's the first time she's stopped talking since we left Canada."

One afternoon in Helsinki, four of us went to the suburbs for a sauna. Eddie McCabe, sports editor of the *Ottawa Journal*, Howie Meeker, and the late Dick Beddoes made the trip. After the sauna we were told that the perfect way to finish it off was to jump in the Gulf of Finland. None of the Finns did it—I guess they knew better than to jump into 40 degree water—but we jumped right in. That may explain why Beddoes always wore a hat, Meeker had that squeaky voice, and, as my friends will insist, I've never been quite the same since.

I had the good fortune to room with Jim Coleman when we got to Moscow. When I was at university, Coleman was writing a sports column for *The Globe and Mail*. I don't think anyone in this country ever did it better.

Coleman had a ritual every morning. We were convinced the rooms were bugged so he gave a daily message to the KGB gumshoes who were listening. "Are you ready?" Coleman said one morning. "I know why you've closed Lenin's tomb. Someone has stolen the body. Brezhnev, why don't you fess up?" I've often wondered, if the KGB had bugged the rooms, what they thought of Coleman's daily diatribes.

The most popular player in Moscow that week was Bobby Hull. Kids would line up to get his autograph and Hull signed for them all. He may have been 5,000 miles from home but Hull was always the autograph hunter's best friend.

The WHA lost the series but no one expected them to win. It wasn't 1972 all over again—that was too much to expect. The hockey lacked the drama of that first summit but all of us, players, press, and fans, had a much better time.

Chapter 6

I'd like to think we'd grown up in two years and realized the fate of the free world didn't really rest on a hockey game. I'd like to think we learned a lot from the Soviets and our game is the better for it. I know they learned a lot from us.

Team Canada won the '72 summit by the narrowest of margins. But the big winner was the game of hockey, which, as we found out, now belongs to the world.

7

Fab Six:

Howe, Beliveau, Hull, Orr, Gretzky, Lemieux

WHO WAS THE GREATEST hockey player I have ever seen? I was fortunate to see everyone from the Rocket to Gretzky and Lemieux. They were all great in their own way.

Rocket Richard was the greatest goal scorer. He played with a passion and fury that no one has ever matched.

Gordie Howe may have been the most complete hockey player because there was nothing that he could not do on the ice. The fact that he was able to play well into his 50s made him unique. His slapshot was the most feared weapon of his time.

Wayne Gretzky was another one who could do it all. He dominated the game when he was on the ice.

Bobby Orr's career was cut short by injuries. As long as he was healthy, there was no one better. He changed the way defencemen played the game for all time. There is no way you can judge how great he would have been if he had remained injury free.

But if I was building a team and could take any player I wanted, I would go for Howe, who was as good defensively as he was offensively.

Gordie Howe scored 801 goals, second on the all-time list in 26 seasons, not to mention his 174 regular season goals in the WHA. But the scoring doesn't tell the whole story of Gordie. The fact he played so well, so long, says it all. He finally packed it in at the age of 52. I can't imagine any of the modern-day players doing it. Wayne Gretzky, the greatest of all time, certainly did not.

A lot of people were kicking themselves for not signing Howe. He was in the New York Rangers training camp as a gangly 15-year-old. Lester Patrick wanted to sign him but Gordie was homesick for his hometown of Floral, Saskatchewan and didn't sign. It is still hard to believe in these days of million-dollar bonuses that Howe signed for a hockey jacket. Jack Adams, the skinflint Red Wings general manager, was happy to give him one. Years later, Howe would move to Houston in the WHA to play on the same team as two of his sons. Howe spent a year with the Omaha farm club and was finally called up by the Red Wings for the

1946–47 season. He was put on a line with Ted Lindsay and Sid Abel the next season. This unit, nicknamed the Production Line, was one of the most successful in the NHL.

Howe's career almost ended before it really started. In the 1950 Stanley Cup Playoffs, Howe took a run at Ted Kennedy, the captain of the Toronto Maple Leafs, and missed, sliding into the boards and fracturing his skull (this was during the time when most players didn't wear helmets). For days he hovered between life and death. It was the last time that he was sidelined by a major injury.

If ever there was a complete hockey player it was Gordie Howe. He could score goals, but also was so tough that no one wanted to have any part of him, which cleared the way for his linemates to score. His elbows, which, contrary to legend he really did not sharpen, were his most lethal weapon, a fact many players soon found out. Such was Howe's reputation that few players were crazy enough to tangle with him.

One who did, Lou Fontinato of the New York Rangers, wound up getting a beating so bad that his bloody face was featured in a three-page photo spread in *Life* magazine. It was not on the actual cover of that issue. In those days, no one worried about hockey being a brutal game, but let's face it, it was.

Off the ice Howe was completely opposite to the nasty player he appeared to be on the ice. In the 1960s I spent a morning with him in Montreal where the Red Wings were playing that night. As we walked the streets, Howe was greeted by hockey fans who were looking for an autograph—this in a city where Howe was conceded to be public enemy number one.

Howe played long enough that his two sons, Mark and Marty, would play on the same team with him, the Houston Aeros of the WHA, first. Mark and Marty then played on the New England Whalers in 1977, which became the Hartford Whalers of the NHL in 1979. A third son decided to pass up hockey to become a doctor, but he was good at the sport, too, playing as a collegiate all-star at the University of Michigan.

Howe decided to jump to the Houston Aeros of the WHA in 1973. The guy who talked him into it was an old rival, Doug Harvey, a Hall of Fame defenceman with Montreal. He sold Howe on leaving the Red Wings front office for the new league because they would allow him to play with his two sons. The boys may not have been chips off the old block but Mark eventually became an all-star defenceman with the Philadelphia Flyers.

Howe eventually played in Hartford, for the Whalers of the WHA, and when the league folded returned to the NHL along with the Hartford club to finish out his career.

Howe had been honoured during a game with Toronto at Maple Leaf Gardens on March 31, 1971, his final appearance there as a Red Wing. In fact, the day was declared Gordie Howe Day. Ballard probably wanted to take the honour back once Howe joined the WHA, as he was livid about losing several players. Saner heads in the Leaf organization convinced Ballard that it would be a terrible mistake not to recognize the greatest player in hockey, especially in a rink where Howe had played so many great games.

Ballard's problems did not end with Howe, he also lost goalie Bernie Parent, to the rival league. Parent did not stay with the WHA and wound up in Philadelphia where he back-stopped the Flyers to two Stanley Cups. "Only Jesus makes more saves than Bernie Parent" was a sign that was displayed in the Spectrum Arena when the Flyers played Buffalo in the Stanley Cup final in 1975.

It's notable that despite losing various players, Ballard honoured Howe. Ballard wasn't known for honouring even his own players that much.

Howe did step out of character that night when he was given a standing ovation in a rink where he had been so often booed: He looked embarrassed by all the adulation. But Howe was far from finished with hockey. Thanks to his wife, Colleen, a brilliant and tough businesswoman, he went into a series of endorsement deals. Every hockey player should have a wife like Howe had in Colleen. In his playing career he was never paid that much money. It wasn't until he went to the WHA that he struck pay dirt, but even then he was never paid what he was really worth.

Howe made up for lost time and then some after he quit playing. He had enjoyed what on the surface seemed like a perfect life. He had a loving wife, even if she did wear the pants, and three sons and a daughter any father could be proud of.

Then it all came crashing down. In the 1990s Colleen came down with a debilitating condition, Pics Disease. She has been confined to her bed, unable to walk or even speak that much. Apparently there is no cure for the disease, at least at the moment. Gordie, after years of renown as a tough hockey player, has been the caregiver, a chore he has performed with loving grace.

The first time I met Jean Beliveau he was playing hockey with the Quebec Aces. He only spoke a few words of English and my interpreter was Punch Imlach, later to be coach of the Toronto Maple Leafs. It wasn't until Punch got to Toronto that I discovered he did not speak any more French than I did. So I got what Imlach wanted me to hear, which was the way he liked to operate.

Beliveau was playing in Quebec, though the Montreal Canadiens would have liked to sign him. Senator Donat Raymond, the owner of the team, was a good friend of Maurice Duplessis, then premier of Quebec. Both men were all too willing to throw their political weight around to keep their star player. Frank Selke Sr., then running the Canadiens, was told that if he signed Beliveau his liquor license would be in jeopardy. The next year, in 1953, the Canadiens did sign

Beliveau, for a salary of $25,000 a year, and Selke retained his liquor license. This seems like petty cash in today's hockey but Beliveau was getting more as a rookie than either Rocket Richard or Mr. Hockey, Gordie Howe. In the 1955–56 season, Beliveau won the scoring title with 47 goals and 41 assists, beating both Howe and Rocket Richard. That year the Habs won their first of five consecutive Stanley Cups. At the time, Beliveau, at six foot four inches, was a giant in a league where six footers were considered huge.

Beliveau succeeded Doug Harvey, the all-star defenceman who had gone to New York to play for and coach the Rangers, as Montreal's captain. At the time, the Canadiens were one of the few teams in the league where the captain was elected by the players. Boom Boom Geoffrion, a 50-goal scorer, felt he should have gotten the job. When it was announced that Beliveau was the choice of his teammates, Geoffrion stormed out of the dressing room and began to fire pucks at the boards.

Beliveau remained captain of the Canadiens for 10 seasons. During his 20 years with the team he scored 507 regular season goals, but that doesn't tell the whole story of his value to the team. He was the inspirational leader of a team that won five straight Stanley Cups.

Beliveau's old coach Imlach decided in 1960 that if the Leafs were to win the Cup, they had to find away to shut down Beliveau. Imlach gave the job to Red Kelly, who had been an all-star defenceman but was switched to centre in order to handle Beliveau. Kelly did not always stop Big Jean but he did such an effective job it played a big role in the Leafs winning the Cup.

When he retired, Beliveau remained with the Canadiens as vice president. He was offered a seat in the Senate by Prime Minister Pierre Trudeau but turned the offer down. He was also considered for governor general but said he was not interested. Beliveau stayed in Montreal, living in the same house across the river in Longueuil that he bought early in his career.

In the 50 years I spent in this business I have never had such a reaction to anything I have written as a story on Bobby Hull that appeared in the *Star Weekly*, a publication of which I was then sports editor. I was not sure anyone paid attention to the text, but accompanying it was a picture of Hull stripped to the waist chucking hay on his farm near Belleville. All of the letters I received were from females young and old who regarded Hull as a sex symbol, the way they now do rock stars.

Hull, of course, was one of the great scorers in the history of hockey. He had five 50-goal seasons in the NHL, and four more in the WHA. In the 1961–62 season he scored 50 goals for the first time, and equalled the record that Rocket Richard had set in the 1944–45 season and that Boom Boom

Geoffrion had equalled in the 1960–61 season. In the final 39 games of that season Hull scored 37 goals.

Actually, Hull would have scored 51 goals in 70 games if not for a goal that was credited to Ab McDonald, then a teammate of Hull's with the Blackhawks. Hull let loose one of his booming drives from just within the blue line and the puck hit a stick. At the time, Hull, along with the referee and goal judge, wasn't sure who the goal belonged to. The goal was credited to Ab, who admitted that his stick never touched the puck. By the time the error was discovered, the report had already gone in to the NHL office and it was too late to change.

One can imagine the uproar in baseball if Roger Maris had hit a home run that was credited to Mickey Mantle. In baseball this is impossible, but in hockey, a faster-moving game where the puck travels quicker than the human eye, mistakes are easily made. Hull was kept from that record, but that was one of the breaks of the game, he said. "I had many other chances for 51 but I blew it."

People like to point out that it took Hull and Geoffrion 70 games to set the record that Richard set in 50 games. But the Rocket had done so in the wartime season of 1944–45 when many NHL stars were off to war, and he never again scored 50 goals.

Hull, like Howe, was more than a hockey player; he was a complete athlete. When the Blackhawks called him up in the fall of 1957 to the big leagues he was still playing fullback for his St. Catharines high school football team.

Chapter 7

Hull scored two touchdowns in his football game that day, and when he got back to the house he was told that Chicago scout Bob Wilson had called. When he sat down, Wilson called again and said, "Hurry down to the rink tonight. The Blackhawks want you to play against the Rangers." That night Hull scored two goals. This was an exhibition game, but it was enough to convince Blackhawks general manager Tommy Ivan to bring him up to the NHL.

That first season Hull scored 13 goals, an impressive mark for a rookie, but he lost out to Frank Mahovlich of the Toronto Maple Leafs for rookie of the year. It is worth noting that Howe also lost out in the rookie voting (for outstanding rookie) and to a Leaf, as well: Howie Meeker. Howe was Hull's boyhood hero and he recalls coming to Toronto when he was about 10 years old and getting an autograph from the Red Wings star after a game at Maple Leaf Gardens. Hull determined then that he would never turn down a request for an autograph and never did, even when it meant keeping the team bus waiting, much to the annoyance of his teammates.

When Hull arrived, the Blackhawks were the sad sacks of hockey and had been in last place for four consecutive seasons. The team was giving away tickets in order to fill the seats. In the 1960–61 season the Blackhawks finally won a Stanley Cup. They upset the heavily favoured Montreal Canadiens in the first round. Hull was badly injured in the series, and though he couldn't take solid food he still played and played well against the Red Wings. Hull got nourishment through a straw from food ground up in a blender. So much for the rap against him that he wasn't nasty enough, a claim Richard had made.

Hull was so strong he didn't have to be nasty. I still recall a game at Maple Leaf Gardens where he picked up Tim Horton, then one of the strongest men in hockey, and held him over the boards.

The big weapon in Hull's arsenal was his slapshot. It's hard to believe, but it was clocked at 119.5 miles per hour. Hull's slapshot was so powerful it knocked down goalies and ripped through gloved hands. Jacques Plante, the backstop for the Canadiens, said, "One of his shots would break my mask. I caught one on my arm and was paralyzed for 15 minutes." The slapshot, which Hull perfected, is by no means a new thing to hockey. Bun Cook was first credited as using a slapshot in the NHL in the 1920s. Though he did not invent it, Hull perfected it and in his hands it became the ultimate weapon in hockey.

From a seat in the stands a spectator could not appreciate the velocity of the shot but Hull spotted me standing back of the net at a Blackhawk practice and decided to have a little fun. Though I was protected by shatterproof glass, when he let loose with his shot, I hit the deck. Later I asked the Blackhawk goalie how he stopped the shot. "There are days you just step aside and leave the door open," was the reply. In those days most of the goalies in the NHL did not wear masks. I can't imagine facing a Hull slapshot without a mask.

I wrote a book on Hull but really never seemed to get under his skin. Well, almost never. Hull was a man who seemed obsessed with money and even threatened to sue me because he claimed he did not know I was writing the book. Fortunately I had sent a copy of the manuscript to him by registered letter and my publisher had his signature on the received slip from the post office.

Hull, of course, signed with the Winnipeg Jets for a million dollars in 1972, a move that made the WHA viable. Bobby Hull has surfaced once again as commissioner of the WHA, which is yet to get off the ground. What they need is a player of Bobby Hull's calibre. Bobby Hull made the WHA. When the Winnipeg Jets signed him he was the biggest star in hockey.

Hull had a volatile relationship with his wife, Joanne, a former figure skater who used to show up at Blackhawk practices in a full-length mink coat. At that time the wives of the other players were wearing parkas. Joanne became so exasperated by Hull when he was in Winnipeg that she took his replica Hart and Art Ross trophies to the pawn shop. Fortunately Bob got a call from the shop owner and was able to retrieve them.

Bobby has passed the torch on to another generation. Brett Hull, Bobby's third son, has joined his father as an all-time great and is a surefire candidate for the Hockey Hall of Fame.

Fab Six

Brett was called up by the Calgary Flames for the Stanley Cup Playoffs against the Montreal Canadiens in 1986, and played two games against the eventual winners. I went into the dressing room and introduced myself to Brett. "I know you," he said, "you wrote a book about my father." Talk about making a guy feel old. I asked Brett if his dad had phoned him after the game. "If I score a couple of goals he might phone," Brett replied, "but if I don't score, forget it."

After the Hull marriage broke up, Brett went to Vancouver with his mother and had little contact with the Golden Jet. Now that he has emerged as a star, he and Bobby are at least talking.

At the time I wrote the book *Bobby Hull*, I rated him as the most exciting player in hockey. I have seen nothing since to change my mind. Gordie Howe was a better all-round player and Hull's scoring record would be shattered, first by Phil Esposito and then by Wayne Gretzky, certainly the best player of the modern era of hockey. But neither Gretzky nor Howe could bring a crowd to its feet the way Hull could. When he was on the ice you just couldn't take your eyes off him.

My son once asked me if I'd ever seen a hockey player better than Gretzky. "Bobby Orr," I shot back without pausing a moment to think about it.

Chapter 7

There's no telling what Orr might have done if his knees hadn't given out, ending his career at the age of 30 in 1978 after only 12 seasons (some of them only partial seasons). But while it lasted there was never anyone who could take charge of a game the way Orr did in the wonderful years he played with the Boston Bruins.

Orr was the Eric Lindros of his day. (Of course Lindros never had the success on the ice that Orr did but, like Orr, he was able to negotiate himself into big contracts. Unlike Orr, Lindros never really lived up to his potential.) Orr took the NHL establishment on and beat them at their own game. It was the making of R. Alan Eagleson, the lawyer who masterminded the deal, that made Orr, at the age of 18, the fourth-highest-paid player in the National Hockey League.

It's hard to believe now when the journeymen players make over a million a season, but in 1966, the year Orr signed with the Bruins, hockey players were the most underpaid athletes in North American sport. Bobby Hull, then the game's leading goal scorer, was being paid $45,000 a season. Gordie Howe, the living legend, who did more things longer than anyone ever to play the game, was paid the princely sum of $40,000 by the Detroit Red Wings. Jean Beliveau got $35,000 from the Montreal Canadiens.

Hockey players had always been at the mercy of management. Under the rules then in effect, the Bruins had the sole right to Orr's services because he played for the Oshawa Generals, a junior team they sponsored. Hap Emms, who never felt hockey players should get much more than the minimum wage, was then running the Bruins. "I can't see any trouble in signing him," Emms said. "He has to prove he can play in this league, then he'll get the big money."

Emms offered Orr $8,000, the same salary as Hull had received eight years before. Emms said he might go as high as $10,000 but no higher. For once he had underestimated his man. The Boston general manager had tried to stop Bobby from playing in the Memorial Cup final against the Edmonton Oil Kings. Orr had a groin injury but doctors told him he could play as long as he could stand the pain. Emms was worried that his million-dollar prospect might suffer a further injury that could hamper him as a pro. He ordered Orr not to play in the final game of the series.

Bobby's father, Doug, wanted his son to play. Doug and Emms met outside the Oshawa dressing room at Maple Leaf Gardens and started to argue. "Mr. Emms," Doug said, "you don't own the boy. I'm his father and I say he'll play."

Bobby did play in a futile attempt to lead Oshawa to the junior championship.

The stage was set for a long summer of tough negotiations. In one corner there was the teenage hockey phenom, his 41-year-old father, who was a $100-a-week packer in a high explosive plant, and Eagleson.

Bobby's father had met Eagleson when they played in the same softball league in Muskoka. He was impressed with the fast-talking young lawyer and hired him to handle the negotiations for his son, who was being hailed as the best young hockey player to come along in years.

In the other corner was Emms, a hockey man of the old school, who in a lifetime of running junior teams had acted as a father figure to his players. Now he was dealing with a youngster who wanted a salary higher than the Bruins had ever paid a player or coach.

Eagleson had a trump card up his sleeve and he played it. Either Orr got what he wanted from the Bruins—a two-year contract plus a bonus—or he would play as an amateur for Canada's national team. It's a similar ploy to the one Lindros was to use a quarter-century later when he refused to sign with the Quebec Nordiques who had taken him in the NHL draft.

The Bruins, who had finished in last place in five of the past six seasons, couldn't afford to wait for Orr. It was the Boston management who had billed the teenager as the million-dollar prospect, the new Eddie Shore. The old one was the Hall of Famer who had been the first big star when the Bruins came to Boston.

I asked Leo Monahan, the hockey writer for the *Boston Record-American*, what the fans would do if Emms didn't sign Orr. "Oh nothing much," he replied. "They'd just riot, burn down the Boston Garden and hang Emms and Weston Adams, the team president, and not in effigy either."

Emms didn't give in easily. Eagleson told me in the middle of August the odds were 60-40 in favour of Orr going to the national team. The Eagle had just asked his client how strong he felt about his stand. "I want to play in the NHL," Orr told him. "But if they don't meet my terms I won't play there."

The Bruins finally gave in. At 1:30 a.m. on a balmy September 1966 night aboard the *Barbara Lynn*, a 42-foot cruiser named after one of Emms's granddaughters, Robert Gordon Orr signed his NHL contract.

To celebrate the occasion, Emms, a teetotaler, cracked open four bottles of Teem, a grapefruit-flavoured drink, and quickly downed them. Orr and his father then adjourned to Eagleson's cottage where they opened a bottle of champagne. Sipping his first alcoholic beverage, Bobby Orr toasted his victory over the NHL establishment.

I had first met Bobby Orr when he was playing for the Oshawa Generals. He's about the shyest person I've ever interviewed. Bobby was just 17 and living in a room in the basement of a house in Oshawa. When I asked a question, Orr looked at the floor before he answered. His replies were usually no more than a couple of sentences at the most.

If ever there was anyone born to play hockey it was Orr. Like Gretzky a decade later he was to dominate every league he played in. The Bruins first spotted him when he was 12, playing in a bantam tournament.

Lynn Patrick, then the Bruins' general manager, was once asked what he saw in the 12-year-old that set him apart. "Oh nothing much," he replied. "He was only skating rings around everyone else on the ice. He had the puck all the time and he played the whole game save for a two-minute penalty."

If anyone had any doubts that Orr was ready for the NHL, they were dispelled when he played against a touring team from the Soviet Union. The 17-year-old Orr dominated the game, easily the best player on the ice for either team.

I recall one night at Maple Leaf Gardens sitting beside Milt Schmidt, the Hall of Fame centre who was then the assistant general manager of the Bruins. "I've been around this game a long time," Schmidt told me, "but I've never seen anyone who could do the things this kid can with the puck."

Orr did more than turn the Bruins, a last-place team, into a Stanley Cup team. He changed the way the game was played. Before Orr came along, the defenceman's job was to stay back and protect the goalie. Orr became a fourth forward, as much a threat to score as anyone on the ice. In the 1970–71 season, when he was at the top of his game, Orr set a record of 139 points—a record that still stands today.

The year before, Orr scored the winning goal against the St. Louis Blues in the Stanley Cup final. A photographer caught Orr flying through the air as the puck went behind goalie Glenn Hall. This famous picture shows Orr at his finest.

Orr was to undergo five knee operations. One of them forced him to sit out the 1972 summit between Canada and the Soviets. I've always thought things would have been a lot easier for Team Canada with Orr on the ice.

Bobby finally got his chance to play for Team Canada against the Soviets in the 1976 Canada Cup. A lot of us think it shortened Orr's career. He played in pain throughout the series, but even on one leg he was better than anyone else on two. He controlled the game, just as he always did.

I'm sure Orr, as well as most of us who watched, knew that this was his last hurrah. He was an almost unanimous choice for the MVP of the series, and it wasn't just sentiment that swayed the voters. Orr was, as he had been throughout his career, the best man on the ice.

The Bruins proved there is no room for sentiment in the cold business of hockey, declining to sign Orr when his contract ran out after the 1975–76 season.

"The Bruins didn't sign me because they thought I couldn't play any more," Bobby said. "They didn't want damaged goods."

Orr wound up going to the Chicago Blackhawks, the start of a downward spiral in both his life and hockey career. He had a bitter parting with Eagleson, the man who had handled his business affairs since he first signed with the Bruins. The two of them, who once were as close as brothers, haven't spoken in years.

Orr played only 20 games in that first season with Chicago. His left knee, the Achilles heel in this otherwise perfect physical specimen, would not let him play any longer.

Bobby was to play only 12 seasons in the NHL. But as long as he lasted, he was the best I've ever seen.

Perhaps the greatest tribute to Orr comes from Larry Bird, the superstar of the Boston Celtics. Bird, who dominated basketball in Boston as Orr once did hockey, was asked why he always seemed to be looking at the rafters in Boston Garden during the playing of the national anthem.

"I look at the banner that honours Bobby Orr," Bird said. "He's the greatest athlete ever to play in this building. I get turned on every time I look up at that banner."

Wayne Gretzky and Mario Lemieux, the two dominant players of their era, could not be less alike. Lemieux, supremely gifted with a tremendous shot, made the game look so easy. Like most great stars you couldn't keep your eyes off him when you watched him play. Gretzky wasn't the most gifted skater or blessed with a great shot, but obviously he could score goals—try 894 of them in his 20 seasons in the league. And at the same time, he made his linemates into scorers with 1,963 assists. There hasn't been a player like him before or since.

Lemieux was always attacked with body checks inside and outside of the rules. Gretzky's opponents did not lay a glove on him, or so it seemed. He was rarely injured in his 20-year career, which may have been because he was so elusive.

Besides, if you hit Gretzky, you knew his teammate Dave Semenko would make you pay for it.

Gretzky wound up in Edmonton almost by accident. Nelson Skalbania had signed him to a personal service contract. When the Oilers joined the NHL they were owned by another entrepreneur, Peter Pocklington. The two men cut cards, or so the story goes, with Pocklington winning and getting the greatest player of his time. Skalbania later said that if he had ever known Gretzky would develop into the superstar he was he would have demanded more for his rights.

Gretzky, like Orr, changed the way the game is played. The Oilers won four Stanley Cups with Gretzky in the 1980s and played a unique, wide-open style of hockey. Fortunately, they had in Grant Fuhr a goaltender who could save their bacon while they were attacking at the other end of the ice.

It's hard for people in Edmonton to accept, but Gretzky was just too big a star for that tiny Canadian city. During the 1988 Stanley Cup Playoffs I wrote a column in the *Toronto Sun* predicting that Gretzky would be traded to the New York Rangers. The column was picked up by the *Edmonton Sun*. That night at the hockey game Terry Jones from the Edmonton paper came up to me and shouted, "Hunt, what have you been smoking! That column today was one of the dumbest I have ever read."

I was wrong about the Rangers team; Gretzky eventually wound up with them much later. Two months after I wrote that column, however, he was traded to the Los Angeles Kings.

Chapter 7

It was a blow not only to Edmonton but to all of Canada. The Oilers could no longer afford to keep their top players. Gretzky, who seemed to have bad luck with owners, was brought to Los Angeles by Bruce McNall, who eventually went to jail for fraud. But at least Wayne got every penny owed to him on his contract. Pocklington had been paying Gretzky $1 million a year, while McNall gave him $8 million a year. Gretzky's salary was the industry's guideline. When he got a substantial raise, every player got bumped up a bit. This started a spiral that culminated in the NHL lockout, with all its salary cap issues, that wiped out the 2004–2005 season.

Gretzky's finest moment with the Kings came when his team upset the Toronto Maple Leafs in seven games and came to play the Montreal Canadiens in the 1993 Stanley Cup final. Even Gretzky could not carry the Kings over the Canadiens, who had Patrick Roy in net, creating a matchup for the ages.

Gretzky finally left the Kings for the St. Louis Blues in the 1995–96 season. The Blues felt Gretzky could get them to the hockey Holy Grail, the Stanley Cup, but they never got there. The next season he signed with the New York Rangers, the team I originally predicted he would go to almost a decade before that. He finished his career with the Rangers, playing his final game on April 18, 1999, not getting a goal but scratching out an assist.

It was a tearful goodbye for Gretzky from a game he not only commanded but that he loved. Since he began to skate on his backyard rink his father had built, hockey became his life. Gretzky left the ice but still had a big role to play in the game. He is one of the owners of the Phoenix Coyotes, a team he hopes to build into a power, though so far they have been life and death to make the playoffs and even to survive financially.

Gretzky was also in charge of putting together the teams that won the gold medal in the 2002 Olympic Games in Salt Lake City and the 2004 World Cup. He had played for Canada in the Nagano Olympics in 1998 where Canada finished out of the medals. They lost in a shootout against the Czechs and Gretzky was not picked to be one of the shooters. This was a tremendous goof by the Canadian coaching staff. He might not have scored on Dominik Hasek, the Czech goaltender, but I sure liked his chances better than those of Brendan Shanahan and Raymond Bourque.

Gretzky is one of the few players in hockey who became big in the United States. I was in New Orleans in the 1990s, hardly a hotbed of hockey, but they had Gretzky 99 jerseys in a sporting goods store—this during Super Bowl week. The success of Gretzky as a merchandiser convinced the NHL that their future was in the Sunbelt cities of the southeastern United States. The Sunbelt teams have not been all that successful, though one of them, Tampa Bay, won the Stanley Cup in 2004. The Sunbelt teams have not been that successful at the box office either, and are more troubling to the NHL because of the lack of television ratings.

Chapter 7

Hockey remains a game in the United States confined to a few northeastern and midwestern teams, all members of the Original Six, plus the Philadelphia Flyers, where the legend of the Broad Street Bullies lives on.

Mario Lemieux has a lot in common with Bobby Orr. Both were prodigious talents and both were plagued by injuries. There is no telling how great Mario might have been if he hadn't been hampered by both injuries and disease. He had a form of cancer, Hodgkin's disease, but battled back and in his first game after finishing his radiation treatments he scored a goal.

I first met Lemieux at the Memorial Cup in Kitchener in 1984. He did not have that great a series, but there was no point talking about it with him. Mario spoke, or at least pretended he spoke, no English. The Pittsburgh Penguins had first pick in the 1984 draft and had numerous offers for Lemieux's rights. The Penguins were a sad sack team, and Lemieux was not at all keen on joining them. He was their first pick, of course, but he declined to put on the Penguins sweater as draft choices normally do. Eddie Johnson, the old goaltender for the Bruins, was the general manager of the Penguins and he said there was no way he would trade Lemieux. "This sort of player comes along once in a lifetime."

Gretzky and Lemieux, then the two biggest stars in the game, finally were on the same line on the 1987 Canada Cup team. It was magic on ice, with Gretzky setting up Lemieux for the winning goal in the championship game against the Soviet Union. Lemieux also starred in the 2002 Olympics and 2004 World Cup.

As I write this, Lemieux is still playing, for a lot of reasons, one of them being that it is the only way he can collect the $12 million owed to him on his contract. To save the Penguins, who were close to bankruptcy, Lemieux became the club's president and partial owner, another first for hockey: the first player, at least in the modern era, to become the chief executive of a team.

The most impressive statistic is that Lemieux (who played in fewer games than Gretzky) has a goals per game rating of .708, while Gretzky achieved only a .601, which shows what a dominant player Mario really is.

Hockey is still looking for the next big star to succeed Lemieux and Gretzky. Eric Lindros, who was once dubbed The Next One, has never realized his potential mainly because of a series of concussions. As I write this I can't think of anyone now playing in the NHL who could take the mantle that Lemieux soon has to discard due to his age and health problems. The closest possibility at present is Junior player Sidney Crosby. Only time will tell if he can rise to the level of Lemieux. I doubt if anyone will ever surpass any of my fabulous six, Howe, Beliveau, Hull, Orr, Gretzky and Lemieux.

The Legends:
From Lionel Conacher to Northern Dancer

I NEVER SAW JACKIE ROBINSON play baseball, Jesse Owens run, or Bobby Jones play a round of golf. But I was fortunate enough to interview them all after their careers were over. I would also include in this list Lionel Conacher, Canada's athlete of the first half of the 20th century.

Bobby Jones was one of the great golfers of all time. He is the only man ever to win the original grand slam. In 1928 he won the British and U.S. Opens and the British and U.S. Amateurs. Then after that he retired, at the age of 28. As an amateur Jones could beat the best in the world and never turned pro because he never saw golf as a real living. He was a successful lawyer and businessman in Atlanta, Georgia.

But what Jones is best remembered for is Augusta National, home of the Masters Golf championship. Jones did play in the early years of the Masters but was never a contender. But it was his name that made the tournament one of the best in golf. By the time I got to the Masters in 1958, Jones was confined to a wheelchair from a crippling disease that would later take his life. He was usually found in a golf cart at Amen Corner watching the golfers play through. Jones made sure that the low amateur had a prominent place in the Masters tournament. He insisted that amateurs be invited, like Canada's Sandy Somerville. He recorded the first ace in tournament history on the 16th hole in the 1936 Masters.

There are a lot of traditions at the Masters that go back to Jones. The tournament is played early in April because this allowed the New York columnists to drop in from spring training. After the play they would all retreat to the veranda and have a few drinks. On the final day they still bring out a bottle or two for the media after the final putt has dropped.

Jones was undoubtedly the greatest amateur of all time and even ranks up there with the best—Jack Nicklaus, Sam Snead, Ben Hogan, and Arnold Palmer.

Jesse Owens was one of the great Olympians of all time. In the 1936 games in Berlin he won four medals. It is one of the legends of that game that Adolph Hitler refused to present any of the medals to Owens. When I met with him in 1949, Owens insisted that this was not true. He explained that the head of state never presented an athlete with medals. Owens never felt snubbed by Hitler but was far angrier about how he was treated when he returned to America. He may have been the best athlete in the world but he was still a black man in a white country.

In 1949 Jesse came to Toronto to run a race against a horse. It was a shame such a great athlete had to do such a ridiculous thing in order to make a living. (By the way, he did beat the horse, just like he did all the two-legged athletes he faced in his career.) I talked to Owens and remember his bitterness towards his own country. One of his great feats was in 1935 at a track meet between Ohio State and Michigan. That day Owens set world records in both the 100 and 200 meter dashes, and in the broad jump. He also ran in the 4 x 100 meter relay.

No athlete in the 20th century played a bigger role than Jackie Robinson, who broke baseball's colour barrier. Jackie was no stranger to Canada. He spent a year with the Montreal Royals of the International League before coming up to the Dodgers. Branch Rickey, who ran the Dodgers, had picked Robinson to be the first black in the major leagues.

When Robinson came to the Dodgers in the spring of 1947, there was considerable prejudice against him. Rickey told him he would have to swallow his pride and let his bat

Chapter 8

do the talking. In a spring training game that year in Florida he slid into home and was met by a sheriff because it was against the law for a black to play on the same field as a white. It was because of Robinson and other black players that the Dodgers set up their own spring training camp at an abandoned air force base at Vero Beach, Florida.

That first season was far from easy for Robinson. The St. Louis Cardinals considered striking rather than playing against him. Saner heads prevailed and they were talked out of it. Robinson's best friend on the Dodgers was Pee Wee Reese, a shortstop from Louisville, Kentucky, which was then a segregationist state. Robinson still was not able to stay with his teammate in hotels that were all reserved for white guests only. It wasn't until Rickey threatened to take the entire team out of the hotel that management let him in.

Robinson paved the way to let other blacks play in the major leagues. In the early days the National League was ahead of the American League in signing black players and that is one of the reasons they dominated for all those years. It is hard to believe that we could have had baseball without Willie Mays, Hank Aaron, Ernie Banks, or Barry Bonds. But if it wasn't for Robinson that could have been a possibility.

I once met Jackie when he came to Toronto to push Chock full o'Nuts coffee. Robinson would have been a great manager but at the time baseball was not ready for a black pilot and so Robinson had to settle for coffee.

The Legends

In any ranking of the great heavyweight fighters of all time, Joe Louis would be up there with the best. Louis is best remembered for his fight against Max Schmeling in 1938. I was 11 years old that summer and living in Sarnia. This was a decade before television, and on that warm night every radio on the street was blaring the fight from Yankee Stadium between the black American and the white German who earlier had given Louis his only defeat in his career. I listened to the fight again recently and I felt the same excitement I felt at the age of 11.

A broadcast of the fight was fed to Nazi Germany, where Hitler and his men stayed up to hear their German Boxer lay a knockout for Aryan supremacy. The Germans never heard their hero get counted out because of a mysterious power outage after Louis laid a body punch that sent the German across the ring screaming. It was one of the most brutal 124 seconds in the history of boxing. Twice the German was knocked to the canvas and struggled up. Schmeling's corner threw in the towel and the fight was stopped. The great Aryan boxer was dismantled by a black man.

After the fight Louis visited the White House, where Franklin Roosevelt told him, "Joe, we need muscles like yours to beat Germany." In his ghostwritten biography Louis mentions the irony that the son of slaves was the one that racist Americans depended on to win the fight.

Chapter 8

Less than three years later the United States was at war. Both Louis and Schmeling joined the army. Louis fought exhibition matches for the soldiers, while Schmeling became a paratrooper and was injured in Crete.

I talked to Louis when he came to Toronto to referee a wrestling match. I last saw him in a bar in a Chicago hotel, sitting alone, nursing a beer. Louis died in 1966, his final years a sad saga of health and financial problems. Schmeling lived to his 80s, a prominent owner of a Coca-Cola bottling plant in Hamburg, Germany. Well into his 90s, he died in 2004.

Jack Dempsey was one of the greats in what has been called the golden age of American sport. Others included Babe Ruth; Bobby Jones; Bill Tilden, the tennis champion; and Red Grange, the great football star. Even among these great athletes, Dempsey stood out as the best of them all. He was the heavyweight champion of the world at a time when the title really meant something.

I first ran into Dempsey in the 1950s. I went to his hotel room to do an interview for *Assignment*, a CBC Radio program. The producer expected we would do one 20-minute item. He turned on his tape recorder and Dempsey just kept talking. It wound up as a five-part series. I had never earned an easier dollar, as Dempsey told of some of the great moments in American sport.

The Legends

There are a few moments I still recall from when Dempsey first spoke of them. There was the fight in 1921 between Dempsey, who did not serve in the First World War, and Georges Carpentier, a French hero of the war. Dempsey knocked him out in four rounds and there was no doubt he was the best fighter on the planet. This was billed as the first fight of the century, and the battle between the draft dodger and the war hero drew a record gate of 80,000, the biggest then in boxing history.

Dempsey recalled that when boxing was banned in New York State, he went to Shelby, Montana to fight Tommy Gibbons. Some Shelby men had wanted to put their town on the map and so scrambled up a $200,000 purse. A wooden bowl for 50,000 spectators was built, but only 7,000 showed up. Right up to fight time there was still doubt that Dempsey and Kearns, his manager, would get their hands on the purse after $50,000 was reneged. Dempsey and Kearns boarded the train with what was left of their guarantee and escaped with it. Boxing has seldom seen such a bizarre incident.

The most sensational fight in Dempsey's career was at the Polo Grounds in New York in 1923 against Luis Firpo, a.k.a. the wild bull of the pampas. Firpo, who outweighed the champ by 24 pounds, knocked Dempsey down early in the fight. In that first round Dempsey went down twice and Firpo five times, making it one of the most explosive rounds in boxing history. Late in the first round Dempsey scored a knockdown. He was convinced that the fight was over, but he was wrong. Firpo responded with an overhand right that knocked Dempsey through the ropes and into the laps of the reporters sitting in the ringside seats. The reporters somehow helped Dempsey get back into the ring, something Dempsey said later that he could not recall.

Dempsey was able to come back in the second round and knock Firpo out, to end the most sensational fight in heavyweight boxing history.

Dempsey finally met his match in Gene Tunney. Their first fight in Philadelphia, on September 23, 1926, drew a crowd of 80,000 and the gate receipts totaled $1,950,733, the biggest in boxing at the time. Tunney was just too fast and clever for Dempsey and wound up getting a unanimous decision and taking the title. Asked by his wife after the fight what happened, Dempsey said, "Honey, I forgot to duck."

Demsey and Tunney met again in 1927 at Soldier Field in Chicago. This fight was carried by 48 radio stations, then the biggest network for any event. The fight almost followed the same script as the first. Dempsey stormed forward and Tunney retreated, throwing counterpunches that cut Dempsey.

In the seventh round Dempsey caught Tunney with a punch to the jaw. He followed up with a flurry of punches and Tunney collapsed and hit the canvas. The referee tried to steer Dempsey to a neutral corner but by the time he had got him there the count had already started. Tunney was on the canvas for at least 14 seconds but was not counted out. He got back up took over the fight and retained his title.

The paid attendance was a 104,933 and the gate totaled $2.6 million, the biggest for a single event in the history of sport at that time.

This was a fight that will always be remembered for the long count that prevented Dempsey from retaining the title. This was to be Dempsey's last fight. Tunney fought for a couple more years, then retired as the undefeated heavyweight champion.

I've interviewed a lot of people but two of the most interesting were both boxers, Dempsey and Muhammad Ali.

Canada's athlete of the first half of the 20th century was Lionel Conacher. Among other claims to fame, he had sparred with Dempsey. Conacher could do it all. Football may have been his best game. He scored 21 points in a 1921 Grey Cup game between the Eskimos and the Argos. He then rushed from the stadium to a waiting taxi that took him to a lacrosse game in Brampton.

Conacher also played in the National Hockey League, winning Stanley Cups with both the Chicago Blackhawks and the Montreal Maroons. He wasn't quite the hockey player his younger brother, Charlie, was, but he was not that far behind. He came from an era when athletes excelled in many sports. But no athlete was as good an athlete as the great Conacher.

I first met Lionel in 1949. He was running for the Liberal Party in that year's election. I met him and his campaign manager, his brother Charlie, in a pub. No one showed up at the scheduled meeting. Lionel will give his speech here, Charlie said, and you can write it as if it was given before a cheering crowd of supporters. He then pulled a $50 bill from his wallet and said, "This is for you." Even though at the time I was only making $35 a week, I told them I could not accept it because I might be fired. "Why not?" Charlie said. "The *Star* is a Liberal newspaper." It was the first and only time I was ever bribed in my career. Even without my help, Lionel was elected, and saved his $50.

Conacher died of a heart attack on May 26, 1954, after hitting a triple in a softball game between Members of Parliament and the press gallery.

I have met a lot of interesting people in my career but one of the most interesting happened to be a horse, named Northern Dancer.

E.P. Taylor, one of the most promising industrialists of his era, happened to own Canada's greatest racehorse. Northern Dancer won the Kentucky Derby on May 2, 1964. It is one of the great moments in Canadian sports that made me wish I was there. I would have been, except no one thought that Northern Dancer, an extremely small horse, had any chance of winning. Of course, he did win and did it in two minutes flat, a time that was later beaten by the great Secretariat.

In any event, I had to do a story on the Dancer after he had won the Derby. Taylor was a busy man, but through a friend of his secretary I was able to arrange an interview at 8 a.m. on a Sunday morning. As I drove to his home on Bayview Avenue, I suddenly realized that I did not have a pen. Luckily, there was a gas station just down the road where I was able to borrow one from the attendant. The half hour I was promised went by quickly and Taylor continued to talk about a horse that had brought him so much joy.

Northern Dancer's diminutive size was the reason he was passed over when Taylor put him up for sale for $25,000. Taylor decided to keep the horse and he admitted he was glad that he had. Northern Dancer was very temperamental. The jockey, Bobby Ussery, rode him in a big pre-Derby race in Hialeah Park. He hit him with the whip and the horse just kept running. It was claimed that before the race, they had Dancer listen to violin solos to calm him down.

I was at Gulfstream Park, Florida in April 1964. The Dancer won and I came home with a pile of cash. Northern Dancer's victory at the Derby was front-page news across Canada and you could make the case it was one of the greatest moments in Canadian sports history. This gallant little horse went on to win the Preakness. Horatio Luro, the trainer, later decided that he did not want to run the horse in the Belmont Stakes due to the long mile-and-a-half course. He was overruled and the colt ran and finished third. Taylor was second-guessed for his decision but had a good excuse. He had lunch three weeks before the race with Queen Elizabeth. The Queen, a horse racing fan, told Taylor that he just had to go for the Triple Crown. Let's face it, no one says no to the Queen.

Northern Dancer was retired to stud and he was to be one of the great sires of all time; his offspring won races all over the world. They say that the Dancer was just as competitive in the breeding stall as on the race track. It is true that he never lost his competitive spirit. The Dancer died in 1990 and his body was brought home to be buried at Windfields Farm, midway between the barn where he was born and the barn where he became a stallion.

9

No Friend of the Maple Leafs:
Pal Hal

ANYONE WHO KNEW HIM, and that includes this author, will agree that Harold Ballard was one of the most unforgettable characters you could ever meet.

You could hate him, or even occasionally love him, but one thing you could never do was ignore the late owner of the Toronto Maple Leafs.

I talked to Ballard hundreds of times. That's not quite true. Most of the time we shouted at each other, with Harold getting in the last word. I'm a match for most big mouths, but with Ballard it was no contest.

I'm not boasting about it, but I did give Ballard the nickname Pal Hal, which was the title of Dick Beddoes' biography of the Leaf owner. The nickname just seemed fitting and, like a lot of nicknames, it stuck.

Chapter 9

I have a special reason for remembering Ballard. He made me famous—perhaps infamous would be a better word—during a post-game TV show at Maple Leaf Gardens. The Leaf owner had been upset at some things I had said on the show the week before. I had suggested that Ballard was a buffoon and he should leave the running of his hockey team to the professional hockey men he hired to do the job.

Ballard demanded equal time and CHCH, the television station that carried the program, was eager to oblige. It was, after all, his building and his hockey team.

I'm sure they weren't prepared for what transpired when Ballard showed up. He had said some outrageous things but usually not on television. Dave Hodge, the host of the program, didn't even get through the introductions before Ballard took over the airwaves.

"We are pleased to have the owner of the Toronto Maple Leafs..." Hodge said.

"Knock it off, Dave," Ballard blurted. "You're not pleased at all. I'm here because I demanded to be here. I'm here to refute the remarks of the bastard you had here last week. I don't want to mention who he is but his last name begins with one of the first three letters of the alphabet."

"Oh, you mean Jim Bunt," Hodge broke in, trying to stop the monologue. He was wasting his breath.

"You're close, Dave," Ballard continued. "You missed by one letter. The letter C."

No Friend of the Maple Leafs

I still find it hard to believe the director didn't bleep so much as a word. Perhaps he was as flabbergasted as everyone on the panel.

Ballard may have thought it was funny. It was an opinion not shared by the members of the Hunt family. My youngest daughter, Kathryn, was in public school. Her classmates didn't take long to pick up on what the Leaf owner had said. "Kathryn, we know what your name rhymes with," they shouted at her in the schoolyard.

I may have been willing to forgive Ballard for what he had said, but my wife, Caroline, was not so forgiving. A few weeks later we met Ballard in the lobby of the Waldorf Astoria Hotel in New York during a series between the NHL and the Soviets.

"Mr. Ballard," she said, "you may have thought what you said was funny. But I'd like you to know how upset it made our 12-year-old daughter. The boys in the schoolyard made her life miserable."

Ballard muttered that he was sorry and slunk away. He couldn't care less what I thought but what my wife said bothered him. I also think he was impressed by anyone who stood up to him. Any time I met him after the incident in New York, he might insult me, which was par for the course, but always asked after my "charming wife."

I didn't understand Ballard. I suspect few other people did either. He could turn on the charm when it suited him but more often was a profane boor.

Chapter 9

The *Toronto Sun*, which felt a Ballard birthday was an event worthy of note, sent me to his cottage in Thunder Bay on July 30, 1988, when he turned 85. Veronica Milne, an attractive photographer at the paper, accompanied me on the trip. We got lost and finally arrived an hour late.

As I walked in the door, Ballard looked at Veronica and said, "Hunt, I know why you're late. You were humping her in the back seat of the car."

Veronica didn't say anything. I suspect she didn't really believe what she had heard. A few minutes later Ballard turned on the charm. After giving us a tour of his cottage he invited us to stay for dinner.

The Ballard household had another couple of guests that night. Harold had found a couple of baby skunks that had been abandoned by their mother. "Ike and Mike," as he called them, nicknames that he gave himself and his late pal King Clancy, were given a haven in the spare bedroom. It was the crusty old owner who got up in the middle of the night to feed them.

I've always felt Ballard related much better to animals than he did to humans. In his later years he seldom went anyplace without TC Puck the wonder dog, who woke up his master each morning with a song.

The dog was given to the Leaf owner by Yolanda, his companion in his final years. Yolanda, who had also been a guest of the government when she was convicted of helping to forge a will, showed up at Ballard's office on one of his previous birthdays. She had baked a cake and insisted on giving it to Harold in person. Yolanda is a very persistent person and finally convinced his secretary to usher her into Ballard's office.

"We have something in common, Harold," she told him as she handed him the cake. "We've both served time." It was the beginning of a relationship that was to last until Ballard's final breath.

It was Yolanda who explained that she had taught the shaggy-haired bouvier to sing for Harold's birthday at the cottage. On Yolanda's cue, the dog—TC stands for Tiger-Cat, a football team Ballard then owned—warbled a few bars while his new master was being photographed blowing out the 85 candles on his cake.

Most men his age were either in the cemetery or trying to find a comfortable seat in the old folks' home. That's not the way Ballard chose to go.

"When they stop asking for your autograph you know it's time to go," Ballard said.

Pal Hal kept a supply of autographed pictures on hand to satisfy the demand. You had your choice of the owner in the uniform of the Toronto Maple Leafs or the Hamilton Tiger-Cats.

Visitors, despite the experience Veronica and I had, shouldn't have had any trouble finding the Ballard cottage. On the flag-pole were the pennants of the Leafs, the Tiger-Cats, and the Hockey Hall of Fame, an institution to which Ballard belonged as one of the builders of the game.

Chapter 9

I had to ask Ballard if there was anything he wanted for his birthday. His reply was vintage Harold.

"I have two of everything except broads," he said, "and I could probably get two of those if I wanted them."

Ballard, though he was plagued by bad health, seldom missed a game that his hockey or football team played. He watched the Leafs from one corner of the Gardens. Getting to the owner's box at Ivor Wynne Stadium in Hamilton was more of a problem. One night Ballard had to be lifted to the upper level of the football park in a crane. I walked into the owner's box that night to talk to Harold Ballard.

"Hunt, I thought you were dead," he shouted.

"Wishful thinking, Harold," I shot back.

The Tiger-Cats beat the hated Argos that night, which in Ballard's eyes made the ascent to his box worth whatever it cost.

Ballard claims he lost a million dollars a year on his football team, which he once, in his usual outrageous fashion, called a bunch of "overpaid losers." The Tiger-Cats made him eat his words when they upset the Argos in the eastern final.

"You guys may still be overpaid," the owner said in the Tiger-Cat dressing room. "But after today no one can call you losers."

I'm certain whatever it cost, Ballard was sure the Tiger-Cats were worth every penny the next week in Vancouver. His football team upset the favoured Edmonton Eskimos 39-15 in the 1986 Grey Cup final.

No Friend of the Maple Leafs

His players carried the owner off the field as he held the trophy over his head. It is one of the ironies of his life that football, a sport he got into as a hobby, would give him what he had been denied for almost 3 decades as owner of the Leafs. That night in Vancouver, Ballard was as happy as I've ever seen him.

Ballard did a lot of classless things in his life. Certainly one of the worst was sending a Gardens employee to pick up Stan Obodiac's car on the morning of Stan's funeral.

No one had served Ballard better and for less money than Obodiac, his public relations director. He was the one who wrote a letter to the *Toronto Star* urging that Ballard be given the Order of Canada. The government of the day didn't heed his plea.

Ballard had trouble firing people face to face. Punch Imlach, brought back by Ballard as the team's general manager in the late 1970s, suffered a heart attack. When he returned to work, his parking spot at the Gardens had been given to someone else. That's how Punch found out he was fired.

Ballard fired Roger Neilson as coach of the Leafs in March of 1979. In typical fashion, Ballard announced the firing to Dick Beddoes during the telecast of a game between the Leafs and Montreal Canadiens.

Darryl Sittler, the Leaf captain, and Jim Gregory, the general manager, met with Ballard and talked him out of it. He agreed to take Neilson back but wanted the coach to appear behind the Leaf bench for the next Leaf game with a bag over his head. Saner heads, primarily Roger's, prevailed. The coach did agree not to take his place behind the bench 'til after the playing of the national anthem. The ploy seemed to inspire the Leafs for at least one game. At the end of the season Neilson was fired and this time it stuck.

The Leafs under Neilson were only a couple of players away from being a Stanley Cup contender. They had knocked off the Islanders in the spring of 1978, losing the semifinals to the Montreal Canadiens. The Islanders, the team the Leafs had beaten, went on to win four Stanley Cups in the 1980s. The Leafs were never as close again under Ballard as they had been that spring of 1978.

I can forgive Ballard for a lot of things. But I can't forgive him, and neither can Leaf fans, for the way he tore down a once-proud hockey team. He turned the best-loved team in Canada into a standing joke. "I won't die till the Leafs win the Stanley Cup," Ballard said. If he had hung around he would have outlived Methuselah.

The last time I saw Ballard was at a Leaf practice during their training camp in Newmarket in September 1989, six months before he died. He shared a chocolate bar with me, though as a diabetic he wasn't supposed to eat candy.

"This is the year we're going to win the Stanley Cup," Ballard said as he had every year since he bought the team.

It was the last time he was to make this prediction. Ballard died on the afternoon of April 11, 1991. The next night his hockey team was to lose to the St. Louis Blues and bow out of the playoffs.

Ballard was at the eye of a hurricane for most of his life. It continued after his death as his children and Yolanda fought. The battling Ballards became the longest running soap opera in Toronto. I suspect Harold would have loved it. At least the Leafs could no longer blame the owner for their continued losses, as they had when Harold was still alive. I had suggested in a column that in his final act in this life Ballard had put a hex on his hockey team.

He was outrageous, bombastic, and even ridiculous. But he was one of a kind and the sports scene in Toronto just hasn't been the same since he left.

10

The Super Bowls:
So Rarely Super

I COVERED 16 SUPER BOWLS and only four of them were good games. All four were played in the state of Florida, but I don't have an explanation for that. It wasn't even called the Super Bowl in the beginning. The first game was just one between the Green Bay Packers and the Kansas City Chiefs. Tickets were only $10 a piece and yet the stadium was only half-filled. The game was televised by both CBS and ABC so you could tune in to the network of your choice. The Green Bay Packers won the game rather handily, 35-10, but Lamar Hunt, who owned the losing Chiefs, got credit for coming up with the name "Super Bowl," which has been in place ever since.

Eventually the NFL was able to fill the stands for the Super Bowl, but they were never able to get the excitement of our Grey Cup.

Chapter 10

The Packers found a new victim in Super Bowl II, the Oakland Raiders, and by nearly the same score: 33-14. If it had not been for Joe Namath, the NFL domination might well have continued and the game may never have become what it is now. By getting a victory in Super Bowl III against the heavily favoured Baltimore Colts, the AFC became a contender. In those early days, the Super Bowl was a competition between the established NFL and the new boys on the street, the AFL.

I should not have been surprised at Namath's bravado. I went to New York in the spring of 1964 to do a story on Namath signing with the New York Jets. At the time the Jets were to pay him $400,000 a year, far more money than any quarterback or any other player was making then. Sonny Werblin, the owner of the Jets, was convinced that Namath was worth every penny and that he would give the new league credibility.

At the time, Namath was in the hospital recovering from the first of many knee surgeries. To my amazement Werblin asked if I wanted to talk to Joe. He phoned the hospital and arranged an appointment shortly after lunch. I walked into the room and saw him in bed with his leg in a cast. After I introduced myself, Namath asked what I would like to drink and pointed to a fully stocked bar. He offered me scotch, a Bloody Mary, a martini, or a Jack Daniel's; I decided to settle for a beer. It was the perfect place to conduct the interview. Namath could not get up and leave so I had him at my mercy.

The Super Bowls

It was a very satisfactory interview. Namath had played at Alabama under the legendary Bear Bryant and he was quite capable of handling the NFL. I got the impression that he was really full of himself, but rightly convinced of his success. Namath turned the Jets, a team whose paycheques often bounced under their previous owner, into one of the most successful franchises in the AFL, soon to be the NFL.

No one should have been surprised by how the Jets played in the Super Bowl. They had already upset the AFL champion Oakland Raiders handily. But no one accepted that they would be any match for Johnny Unitas and the Colts. But when Unitas got hurt, Earl Morrall proved to be a satisfactory replacement. The Colts were 21-point favourites and the Jets were not expected to even come close.

On the Thursday before the game, Namath made a speech to a sales club in Fort Lauderdale, Florida, where he guaranteed the Jets would win. It was only a few miles from where Muhammad Ali had famously foretold that he would beat Sonny Liston for the Heavyweight Championship in 1964. At the time no one took Namath seriously, certainly not the Colts, who laughed off his bravado, or the nation's sportswriters, who gave Namath and the Jets little chance. Namath insisted after the game he was not just shooting off his mouth when he made his guarantee. I'm not so sure I believe him, but the Jets did win the football game 16-7. It was won by their defence, who shut down Morrall and then Unitas who came off the bench in the second half. Namath was not the only big winner. Dave Anderson, who covered the Jets for the *New York Times*, wrote Namath's fame into a book and eventually into a job as a sports columnist for his paper, the most prestigious paper in the United States.

The first Super Bowl I ever covered was in Houston between the Miami Dolphins and the Minnesota Vikings in 1974. The game was played in a rather rundown facility by the name of Rice Stadium. The Astrodome was a much superior stadium but was considered too small for the game, but perfect for Commissioner Pete Rozelle's party. At that time it seemed everyone was invited to this lavish affair. The owners sat in an enclosure with bodyguards keeping away the rabble.

The game itself was not that memorable. The Dolphins beat the Vikings, the second of four times that Minnesota, coached by my good friend Bud Grant, was to lose the Super Bowl. The Dolphins just ran the Vikings into the ground. Minnesota's defensive line was not big enough or strong enough to handle Larry Csonka and Jim Kiick, Miami's one-two running punch.

Grant sure was a bear for punishment. The next year in New Orleans the Vikings were back again, this time to play the Pittsburgh Steelers. The Steelers had their famed steel curtain defence that only allowed six points, keeping the Vikings south of the end zone. But for someone like me who had picked and bet on the Vikings, it was nice to see 80-year-old Dan Rooney finally win a Super Bowl. He had bought the Steelers with money he won in the 1930s betting on a horse race. The NFL obviously wasn't as nervous about people betting on games as they became in later years.

In 1976 we finally got a Super Bowl that actually lived up to its name. The Pittsburgh Steelers again won, but this time with an offence featuring QB Terry Bradshaw and wide receiver Lynn Swann. The Cowboys made a game of it and were driving for the winning touchdown when time ran out. This was a game worth remembering, but so were the pre-game press conferences. Hollywood Henderson, a linebacker for the Dallas Cowboys, said that Steelers QB Terry Bradshaw could not spell cat, even if you spotted him the C and the A. Bradshaw had the last laugh thanks to the Pittsburgh win, and the next time Hollywood was in the news it was for using drugs. The Cowboys QB Roger Staubach, a straight shooter if there ever was one, surprised us all by saying he had more sex than Namath. Staubach later explained it was all with his wife. Fortunately, as long as the Cowboys and the Steelers kept playing, the quotes from the stars were not the big thing at the Super Bowl.

The next big Super Bowl was in 1979, also between the Steelers and the Cowboys, in the Orange Bowl Stadium in Miami. The stadium seemed to bring the best out of both teams and the NFL did their best to treat the media well. They were determined that more writers and broadcasters would cover the Super Bowl than baseball's World Series. We were given box lunches that included lobster and rare roast beef, as well as a bottle of white wine to wash them down with. At the '79 Super Bowl Ethel Kennedy, the widow of the slain senator, was lining up to go to the ladies' room in the press box. Rank does have its privileges, since the press box lineups were much smaller than those of the public areas. It all made up for a series of rather boring football games.

No one could complain about the 1979 game being a bore. The Steelers won this one, their third championship of the decade. I was standing behind the Dallas Cheerleaders, which is not a bad place to watch the football game from, when the Cowboys scored what appeared to be the winning touchdown. Staubach threw a pass to the usually sure-handed Jackie Smith, but for some reason he dropped it and Pittsburgh held on, winning 35-31. I still think this game is the best of the 16 Super Bowls I covered.

Some teams just could not handle the Super Bowl: the Vikings, of course, the Denver Broncos, who broke their losing streak in 1998, and the Buffalo Bills, who lost four straight. The Broncos lost in 1978 to Dallas in New Orleans, to the New York Giants in the 1987 Super Bowl game at the Rose Bowl in Pasadena, and then to the Washington Redskins in San Diego the following year. This was the game where Doug Williams became the first black quarterback not only to win the game but also to take MVP honours. Williams was asked if he had always been a black quarterback. He looked at the questioner and politely answered, "Yes." Dexter Manley, later a CFLer with Ottawa, insisted he would only answer questions given to him in writing. Funny, because Dexter was illiterate.

The Broncos, who kept on showing up despite their terrible record, were back in 1990 in New Orleans. This time, tickets, which started at $10 in the first Super Bowl, were now selling at $125. This was the game when Joe Montana and Jerry Rice again proved an unstoppable combination and Elway was once again in the losing dressing room. After the game, Elway appeared in a bathrobe looking like Sonny Liston the day Muhammad Ali KO'd him. This Super Bowl did produce my favourite story.

Bubba Paris was an offensive tackle for the 49ers. I just happened to be walking by when Bubba shared a story that was hard to believe. He was in bed with a young lady and decided then to get his life in order. He had jetted out of bed and called a preacher, leaving the startled lady lying there, and then had gone to church to confess his sins. It just had to be said, Bubba said. The next day Bubba had a bigger group of reporters around him than did Joe Montana, the 49ers quarterback.

It's just a coincidence that the two coaches with the worst Super Bowl records both coached in Canada. Grant, who lost four with the Vikings, won four Grey Cups with the Winnipeg Blue Bombers. Marv Levy, who lost with the Bills, won two of our national championships with the Montreal Alouettes.

I still think that if the Bills had beaten the New York Giants in their first trip to the Super Bowl, they might have won two or three more. They were the better team in that 1991 game in Tampa. But defence usually wins big games and it certainly did for the Giants that day. Their defence was masterminded by Bill Belichick, who later won three Super Bowls of his own. The Bills K-gun offence, which had blitzed the AFC during the regular season, was kicked by the Giants. They beat up on the Oakland Raiders in the AFC championship game so decisively that Al Davis, the Raiders owner, stormed out of the press box in disgust. Scott Norwood was blamed for missing a 40-yard field goal that would have won the game. It just missed wide right and Norwood became the scapegoat, especially on talk radio in Buffalo.

At least Norwood was luckier than a former kicker for the Bills. Ralph Wilson, the owner of the team, told some reporters one day that in the old days of the AFL his kicker missed a field goal that would have won the game. On the way home from the stadium, then in downtown Buffalo, the kicker was pulled out of his car and beaten up. "Did you call the police?" Wilson asked the kicker. "No," he replied, "I deserved to be beaten up."

A lot of nutty things happened to the Bills in their next three trips to the Super Bowl, none of which they came even close to winning. In 1993 against Dallas, Thurman Thomas lost his helmet and had to miss a series of downs. The Bills were certainly unlucky in the Super Bowl—or, in some cases, outclassed. They came back again to play Dallas and got the same result. This time Buffalo fans took out their anger on

Jim Kelly, the quarterback. In bars where they were watching the game on television, they cheered when Kelly was carted off the field in a stretcher. Hell hath no fury like a football fan who sees his bets get sucked down the drain.

In its early days the Super Bowl was just a football game. Fans could afford to go to the game and get tickets. In recent years it has become an event for corporate America. Most of the tickets end up in the hands of the sponsors who make the NFL engine purr. The game is now an event staged for television. I don't now how many people will even remember that the New England Patriots won the 2004 game. The big story was Janet Jackson exposing her right breast on the live halftime show. I don't know how many people saw the incident. I didn't, but my aging eyes are not what they used to be. But the media made it the story of the game and that was unfortunate, especially for a game of that calibre.

Someday the NFL may come to Canada; I just hope it is not in my lifetime. I'm afraid it would mean the end of the Argos and the CFL, and I would never want to see that happen. Paul Godfrey, the former chairman of Metro Toronto, who is still dining out on bringing the Blue Jays to Toronto, thinks he will get an NFL franchise. I bet Godfrey, who was then my boss at the *Sun*, a dinner that there would not be a team in Toronto by the end of the '90s. The millennium came and then went and I'm still waiting to collect my dinner. Even Godfrey will admit when he's pinned down that Toronto is no closer to getting a team than it ever was.

There are a few things I want to get off my chest about the Super Bowls I have covered.

The best teams? A toss-up between the Steelers of the '70s and the 49ers of the '80s. They both won four Super Bowls. The Steelers, with Terry Bradshaw, and the 49ers, with Joe Montana, had the two greatest quarterbacks in the history of the game. I'm leaning towards the 49ers but if the two men had ever met in their prime it would have been one amazing game.

The Steel Curtain vs. Joe Montana would have been one for the ages. As you may have guessed, Montana gets my vote as the best quarterback to ever play in a Super Bowl. Namath doesn't make the cut because he only played in one game. I'm also ruling out Johnny Unitas, who never got the chance to really play in the big game. Unitas did play in the 1958 NFL championship game between the New York Giants and his Baltimore Colts. The Colts won it, on an overtime touchdown by Allen Ameche.

That game produced one of the more intriguing stories I have come across. Lou Chesler, a Toronto-based mining promoter, had a piece of the Colts. He had bet $100,000 on the game and had given five points. The Colts had to win by a touchdown to bail him out. So the story was that Chesler appealed to Carroll Rosenbloom, primary owner of the Colts who was also a high roller, to order Unitas to go for the TD rather than the almost-sure field goal that would have won the game. That winter, Unitas was at a sports celebrity dinner in Toronto. I was brash enough to ask him about the story. Johnny admitted he had heard it but insisted there wasn't a grain of truth to it. "How would you like to go into a huddle and tell the guys we had that you were going for a touchdown because the owner wanted it? They would have kicked the crap out of me." Sure, it was a chip-shot field goal, but even they could be blocked.

11

Dopes and Hopes:
Canada in the Olympics

THE FIRST SUMMER Olympics I covered were the 1964 games in Tokyo. It was a wonderful experience. The Japanese did everything in their power to make it a near-perfect event. In the morning sessions, Japanese school children filled the stadium. When they left, there was no litter as would be found in stadiums across North America. Security was not a major issue at these games. Reporters could walk into the Olympic Village whenever they wanted. All they had to do was leave their media pass at the gate. Of course, this was before the 1972 Games in Munich, which changed the Olympics forever. After the massacre of the Israeli athletes, security became a prime concern, and a prime expense at that.

One of most interesting things in the village was the Australian huts, which were littered with cartons of beer, but that did not stop them from winning medals. One of the Aussies jumped in the moat outside the Emperor's Palace, which is a no-no, but she was not arrested. The first two Canadians to win a medal were rowers George Hungerford and Roger Jackson. Harry Jerome, the 100 meter sprinter who had pulled up lame in the Games in Rome, was able to redeem himself in Tokyo. He did not win the gold, however. That belonged to Bob Hayes of the United States, who won it in world-record time. Jerome took the bronze.

I finally caught up to our championship rowers on the day after their win. I talked to them in their hut in the Olympic Village, sitting on one of their bunks. Jackson later told me that I was the first Canadian journalist to interview them. It's hard to believe, in this era where any Canadian with hope of a medal is interviewed countless times. But this was not that era and rowing was still not a glamour event. It became one later due to the success of Canadians in the sport.

There were a few outstanding moments at those games. Canada's Bill Crothers ran second in the 800 meter event to New Zealand's Peter Snell. Crothers was later to get even with Snell when he beat him in a race at Varsity Stadium in Toronto. It produced a crowd of 18,000, the biggest at the time to witness a track event in Toronto. Crothers was not the star of Canada's track team. That honour belonged to Bruce Kidd, a middle distance runner. But Kidd failed to make the finals in any of his events and on the last day went to Hiroshima, the site of the first atomic bomb.

Dopes and Hopes

Because of the time difference between Toronto and Tokyo, when the events were taking place it was the middle of the night back home. It really did not matter since the TV events were shown a day later. The Canadian media were not nearly as critical of Canadian athletes as they became later. Perhaps we just did not expect much from them. Crothers' silver and the gold in rowing were celebrated as achievements.

If I had to come up with an outstanding performance of these games, it would go to a marathoner from Ethiopia. Abebe Bikila had won in his bare feet in Rome four years earlier. This time he wore shoes and after coasting to victory did a victory lap and then dropped down and did 50 push-ups in the infield. He symbolized what the Olympic moment was all about.

Tokyo was an incident-free Olympics. If anyone was using drugs, we were not any the wiser. And Munich, where the world was changed forever with the massacre of the Israeli athletes, was two Olympiads away.

It's unfortunate that the 1976 Olympics in Montreal are remembered for the massive debt that they incurred. The games themselves were both a financial and artistic success. But you can hardly overlook the billion-dollar deficit that was run up mainly in the building of the Olympic Stadium. The Quebec government attempted to pay off the debt by creating a cigarette tax, which is ironic since smoking is now banned in the "Big O," as the stadium is referred to. I was in

Chapter 11

Montreal in June 1976 and thought there was no way the contractors were going to finish the stadium on time. They did eventually finish it, but at a cost. The contractors took advantage of the situation, with vast overruns. One contractor was caught taking out excavated material in a truck and bringing it back in again in the attempt to be paid twice. None of the contractors went to jail, though they should have. It was the price Montreal was willing to pay in order to complete the stadium.

All that was forgotten when the games opened. I was in the stadium that day when Her Majesty Queen Elizabeth declared the games opened. It was one of those days when you were proud to be Canadian. The stadium was still not completed, though. The plastic roof had not been built and was not constructed on the stadium for another three years. Montreal paid a massive price for the games, with a stadium that never really suited their baseball Expos, or their football Alouettes. Now the Expos are gone completely (reincarnated as the Washington Nationals), and the Alouettes are in their own stadium, Percival Molson Memorial Stadium, built just for football at McGill University. The Olympic movement owes a debt of gratitude to Montreal, though. After the killing of Israeli athletes in Munich in 1972, not many cities were willing to take on the Olympics. Montreal did and put on a fabulous show.

These were one of the first games when security became a major item and a major expense. The Olympic Village was no longer the wide-open place it had once been. But all that security did not stop a journalist from the *Star*, Rosie DiManno. She snuck into the village and marched in the opening ceremonies with the Canadian team. No one was any the wiser until the *Star* published the journalist's story.

Canada had the dubious distinction of being the only host country in the history of the Olympics not to win a gold medal during *their* Olympics. Canada only took home two silver medals, one in track and the other in horse jumping. This came as a massive disappointment for the Canadian Olympic team who were competing on their home soil. As it turned out, Canada might have won medals in swimming. But the East Germans, who cleaned up in the pool, were using steroids long before the world discovered them. That was really the big story of the games but no one reported it. An American swimmer, Shirley Babashoff, complained that the East Germans who beat her were not actually women. But she was brushed off as another American complaining. Canadian journalists who should have known better even hailed the East German success. They compared that country, with a population of less than 10 million, with Canada. What they failed to understand was that their success came from a needle.

The individual star of these games was the Romanian gymnast Nadia Comaneci; she became the first gymnast in the history of the Olympic Games to receive perfect 10 scores. The gymnastics were held at the Forum and became a hotter ticket than Montreal Canadiens hockey games that were usually played there.

Cuba also played a dominant part in the games, to the dismay of the Americans. Alberto Juantorena won both the 400 and 800 meter races in record time. He had to share the spotlight with boxer Teofilo Stevenson, who took home the gold in the heavyweight division. The Americans dominated boxing, taking six gold medals. This was an American team that included "Sugar" Ray Leonard; the Spinks brothers, Harold and Leon; and Howard Davis, all of them going on to have great success in pro careers.

The Americans did not even get a bronze in the 100 meters. Hasely Crawford of Trinidad won, with Donald Quarrie of Jamaica taking silver. Quarrie then went on to win the 200 meter event, where the Americans were shut out once again. Finland's Lasse Viren won both the five and ten thousand meters. He had performed this feat in 1972 as well, setting Olympic records in both events. Viren was accused of blood doping, a charge he did not really deny. But there was no such thing as drug testing at the Montreal games. The Americans did not get the harvest of medals they expected but did win the decathlon and the title of the world's greatest athlete. Bruce Jenner followed up the title with a number of endorsements, which made his bank account the big winner.

The Olympics were a big disappointment for Canada from an athletic standpoint. The federal government set up

This was taken in 1961, the year Mickey Mantle (left) and Roger Maris went head to head for the homerun record. Maris got it. Mantle was an interesting person—a complete nut—but a magnificent athlete all the same. (Photo by Harold Barkley, courtesy of Jim Hunt.)

When Brooks Robinson played for the Baltimore Orioles (1955-77), he was considered the best third baseman in baseball, winning 16 Golden Glove awards—the record for any player in any position. In local news, Brooks married a girl from Toronto. (Photo courtesy of Jim Hunt.)

In the press box at the Grey Cup. Me in the centre in the checked coat with Jim Coleman behind, in glasses.
(Photo courtesy of Jim Hunt.)

I interviewed Casey Stengel during spring training in St. Petersburg, Florida, in 1962, his first season managing the Mets. The Mets were an expansion team at the time—they didn't have a chance, finishing last in the league, but he was still inducted into the New York Mets Hall of Fame in 1981, as well as the Baseball Hall of Fame in 1966. (Photo by Harold Barkley, courtesy of Jim Hunt.)

Bernie Faloney was the quarterback for the Hamilton Tiger-Cats in the 1960s when this photo was taken. He led the Ticats to two Grey Cups in the late 50s and early 60s after first winning the Cup in his rookie year with the Edmonton Eskimos. He finished his career with the Montreal Alouettes. (Photo courtesy of Jim Hunt.)

With Nancy Greene at the Toronto City Hall reception in her honour. She was just returning from the 1968 Grenoble Olympics as gold medallist for Canada in downhill skiing, and I was there to interview her for CKEY radio. She was a wonderful person; still is. (Photo courtesy of Jim Hunt.)

Penny Tweedie, right, was the owner of Secretariat, the great Triple Crown–winning racehorse. Here she's being interviewed by the *Globe and Mail*'s sports columnist Dick Beddoes in 1973 (me on the left), in the walking ring at Woodbine racetrack just before Secretariat ran the last race of his career, the Canadian International Stakes. He won. (Photo courtesy of Jim Hunt.)

Here's me in Red Square in Moscow in 1972, while I was over there covering the Canada-Soviet Union summit series. (Photo courtesy of Jim Hunt.)

a sports ministry in order to get amateur athletics back on track. We did not find out what the result of this action was in 1980 in Moscow because Canada decided to join in the American boycott of the games. But the 1984 Olympics in Los Angeles were Canada's best, though it should be pointed out that the Communist countries did not attend, as a payback to the Americans. Who knows what would have happened if they had showed up, but it was still a great success for Canada.

One of the great moments for Canada in the Olympics should have been Ben Johnson's win in the 100 meters at Seoul. He demolished the field in world-record time. But no one remembers the race. Ben was caught with steroids and his medal was taken away. He has always insisted he was not the only one on drugs in that Olympics. He is probably right, but Ben was the only one caught. The Johnson incident overshadowed what should have been another great Canadian moment. Boxer Lennox Lewis won gold in boxing in the super heavyweight division. Lennox later went on to win the heavyweight championship as Joe Frazer and Ali did before him.

Perhaps Canadians overreacted to the Johnson incident, for example when our Olympic brass decided to implement the toughest drug testing of any nation in the world. Canada came back with another 100 meter champion, Donovan Bailey, at the Atlanta games in 1996. He ran the 100 meters in world-record time and no one even suggested he was on drugs. Since he was a Canadian he was tested so often that he had to be clean. Bailey also anchored Canada to a 4 x 100 meter gold, another event that the Americans usually dominated.

Atlanta was the best showing as a complete Olympics by Canada. We won 22 medals and most of the gold came in marquee events. The 2000 Olympics in Sydney were not as successful. Simon Whitfield won a surprise gold in the triathlon but that did not make up for our poor showing. The 14 medals we won were below our expectations but perhaps we asked too much of our athletes. We do not pour the money into athletics the way the Aussies do, so why should we expect that kind of success? Nonetheless, the Aussies won 15 swimming medals at the 2004 Olympic Games in Athens, while Canada, once considered a swimming power, was shut out completely.

Canada has had more than its share of Olympic heroes. Percy Williams, the first great hero for medals, won both the 100 and 200 meter events in the 1928 games in Amsterdam. These summer games were the first games in which female athletes were permitted to compete. The Canadian women took advantage and dominated the track and field events. Bobby Rosenfeld, Canada's female athlete of the half century, anchored the Canadian relay team to the gold medal. Ethel Catherwood won the high jump. At the time, Canada's female athletes were ahead of the rest of the world.

In the 1932 Olympics in Los Angeles, Percy Williams was unable to repeat in the sprints and finished out of the medals. It turned out that Canada's only gold medal in track and field came as a big surprise in the form of Dunc McNaughton of Vancouver, who was not invited to be a member of the team. He was going to University of California where he was a member of the track team as a high jumper. He was a walk-on for the Olympics and wound up winning the gold medal.

It was the first time Canada won a medal that no one expected. It seems that these days most of our medals fit that category. Hilda Strike of Canada finished second in the 100 meter dash at the Games in 1932 in Los Angeles and was still the fastest woman in the race. It turned out that the Polish runner who won, Stella Walasiewicz, was not a woman but was just a cross-dressing man. German doctors who examined her at the time said she was male, but an autopsy would later reveal that she was intersexed, with both male and female genitalia. She was nicknamed "Stella the Fella" but was only stripped of her dignity, not her gold medal.

It's no surprise that Canada has always shown better at the Winter Games. The 1988 Games in Calgary, a financial and artistic success, not only produced medals but the venues for our athletes to train. The upcoming Winter Games in 2010, which have been awarded to Vancouver, will hopefully continue Canada's great Olympic spirit and perhaps even see our Canadian team take the overall medal lead.

12

Covering Baseball:
Maris, Mantle, and the Babe

I'VE BEEN LUCKY ENOUGH to see most of the great ballplayers of the last century, from Babe Ruth to Joe DiMaggio to Ted Williams. I'll confess that I was only seven years old when I saw Ruth in 1934, his last season with the New York Yankees. I was taken to Detroit as a reward for behaving myself when I had my tonsils removed. I don't remember much about that game except that Ruth struck out three times and that Schoolboy Rowe, the Tiger pitcher, hit a home run.

I have always wished that I could have seen Ruth, the greatest hitter of all time, in his prime. He was the first to hit 60 home runs in a season, a record that stood for over 30 years, until it was broken in 1961 by Roger Maris, another Yankee slugger.

Chapter 12

But the Babe is still remembered for the curse he supposedly put on his old team, the Boston Red Sox. Ruth, a left-handed pitcher as well as slugger, was sold to the Yankees by the owner of the Red Sox to invest in a musical, *No, No, Nanette*. It is a fact that the Red Sox had never won a World Series since 1918 until they won in 2004. I was in Shea Stadium in 1986 to see the curse at work when Bill Buckner let a ball dribble through his legs to cost the Red Sox the World Series against the New York Mets.

I was also fortunate enough to see Lou Gehrig, the Babe's "Murderer's Row" teammate. I once got a ball from Gehrig when he handed it to me during a game. Gehrig was a real tightwad, though. When Gehrig and the Babe would eat together, Gehrig would leave a tip of a nickel, which the Babe substituted with two quarters. Gehrig is best remembered now by the disease that is named after him, one that eventually took his life. But he was a great ballplayer even if he was overshadowed by the flamboyant Ruth. The disease also ended Gehrig's streak of 2,130 games, which earned him the nickname "the Iron Horse." The streak was eventually broken by Cal Ripken Jr. of the Baltimore Orioles in the 1990s.

Getting back to Babe, Ruth always dreamed of being the Yankee bench boss. Yet Ruth could hardly discipline himself let alone the New York Yankees. Ruth spent his final years with the Pittsburgh Pirates and the Boston Braves, but he was anything but happy. He was out of shape and his lavish lifestyle of wine, women, and cigars had finally caught up with him. Babe died of throat cancer in 1948. His funeral service was in St. Patrick's Cathedral, his last appearance in a city he once owned. It was a steamy August day and Waite Hoyt, one of his former teammates, said he could use a cold beer. "So could the Babe," replied another Yankee player. This reminds me of a visit I made to New York City in 1956 to do a story on Mickey Mantle. I was waiting to get my press credentials when a middle-aged woman walked past on the way to the elevator at Yankee Stadium. It was Babe Ruth's widow on her way to the bar in the Stadium Club.

The Yankees have always managed to come up with some of the greatest stars in baseball. Ruth and Gehrig gave way to DiMaggio, who joined the Yankees in the 1936 season and led them to the World Series. When you think of DiMaggio you also think of Ted Williams, his great rival. I have a prejudice against DiMaggio and I'll admit it. During his career he did terrible things to my favourite team, the Detroit Tigers. But Williams was my favourite ballplayer. Sure he was difficult and if I had been a newspaper man in Boston I wouldn't have liked him much either. But he was the greatest hitter of his time.

The 1941 season may have been one of the greatest in the history of baseball. That was the year that DiMaggio hit safely in 56 straight games, a record that still stands. It is an old cliché that records are made to be broken. But no one has ever come within 12 games of the record and to this day it seems untouchable.

Chapter 12

That was also the year that Williams hit .406, the last time a major league player hit over .400. But DiMaggio still won the American League MVP award, with Williams finishing a close second in the voting of the baseball writers. Unlike Williams, DiMaggio was a great buddy of the New York sports reporters. He would sometimes give an interview over a fancy meal.

I have many good memories of Williams. One is of a time after the war when Williams returned after a stint as a fighter pilot in the Marine Corps. I was sitting in the press box when Fred Hutchinson, the pitcher for the Tigers, threw a sinker to Williams at the knee and Williams slugged it into the upper deck of Tiger Stadium. I will never forget the look on Hutchinson's face. He told me that he threw a perfect pitch and Williams still hit a homer.

Williams loved to hit in Tiger Stadium. They still talk about the home run that he slugged in the 1951 All-Star Game in Detroit. That game may have been his big stage but in the World Series he was a bust. In his only World Series, against the St. Louis Cardinals, Williams hit a puny .200. There is no telling what Ted could have been if the Second World War had not taken up three of his prime years. There is good reason to think he might have hit .400 again.

Williams lost another two years from his career when he was recalled as a pilot for the Korean War. He had to live a charmed life to walk away from a crash of his jet fighter when it was badly damaged by enemy fire but left Williams without a scratch.

Williams offered to take a pay cut in his later years. He was making $100,000 a year and offered to take a 25-percent reduction. If he had tried that today he would have been hung from the highest tree by the players' union.

It is typical of Williams that he did not linger on like so many athletes normally do, when their best years are already behind them. In his final game, on September 28, 1960, only 10,454 showed up to bid farewell to the greatest hitter of all time. On what was to be his final at bat, Williams hit a home run. He then disappeared into the dugout and, also typical of Ted, refused to come out to be applauded by the few fans in the park. As novelist John Updike wrote, "Gods do not answer letters." Williams left the game with his 521 home runs, leaving him, at the time, behind only Babe Ruth and Jimmy Foxx on the all-time list.

Williams, unlike Ruth, got a chance to manage a major league team. Great players seldom make good managers, though, because they are too demanding. Ted lasted a little more than a year with the Washington Senators, who were a terrible team. The team was managed by the greatest hitter of all time yet had the lowest overall batting average in the league. The All-Star Game was in Washington that year, 1956, and Williams and his old rival DiMaggio hooked up once again. DiMaggio was honoured at a dinner as the greatest living ballplayer. Williams was invited to be awarded with a plaque as the greatest living hitter. Williams took it as an insult and never showed up. Williams was not an easy man to get along with even after he joined the all-time greats in the Hall of Fame as an automatic first-round selection.

One year my youngest son, Andrew, then 12 years old, was with me at a spring training game between the Boston Red Sox and the Toronto Blue Jays. Andrew was sitting on a bench watching the game and who should walk up and sit down beside him but Ted Williams. Andrew once told me that it was the most interesting conversation he had ever had and that Williams, even with his 51-year-old eyes, could still call a pitch after it left the pitcher's hand from nearly 100 feet away.

One of the last times the two greats, DiMaggio and Williams, appeared together was at the 1991 All-Star Game in Toronto. The fans gave them a standing ovation and then decided to boo the prime minister, Brian Mulroney. Williams died after a series of strokes in July of 2002. But Ted was not to rest in peace, because of his dysfunctional family, who later froze him right beside Walt Disney in an Arizona lab. A disgraceful end. There may be better hitters to come along in later years but I doubt I will ever see one.

As kids growing up in Sarnia my brothers and I were such hardened Tiger fans that we named our dog Mickey after Mickey Cochrane, the Tigers manager. The Tigers beat out the Yankees for the Pennant in 1934, losing the World Series to the St. Louis Cardinals. The next season the Tigers won the series over the Chicago Cubs, also a team that seemed to have a curse hanging over their heads.

Covering Baseball

The World Series was then played in the afternoon. We taught our grandmother to keep score. She listened to the games on the radio and when we got home from school we could find out what happened in the game. The Tigers did not get into another World Series until 1940 when they played the Cincinnati Reds. That was the year Buck Newsome put on one of the greatest pitching performances in series history. He won three games but it still was not enough to save the Tigers.

My father was at the series and brought my brothers and me home a baseball autographed by Newsome. My brothers and I first decided to play catch with the ball and then moved on to hitting it. We eventually scuffed up the ball so that the autograph was barely visible. But autographs were not all the rage back then, or so I'd like to think. If I really want to kick myself, though, I just have to recall a ball autographed by Mickey Mantle and Roger Maris now worth a fortune, which I gave away to a neighbour's son. I don't know what ever happened to it, I just hope he did not sell it.

Roger Maris and Mickey Mantle became an item in the summer of 1961 when the two sluggers launched an attack on the most famous record in baseball. Mantle was a star from the day he joined the Yankees. He played the 1951 season in left field with Joe DiMaggio. DiMaggio resented the up-and-comer and did little to help him. In the World Series that season, Mickey was chasing a fly ball and stepped in a drain hole and injured his knee. It was the first of many injuries that would plague Mantle for the rest of his career.

Mantle was famous for his tape measure home runs. In 1956 he won the Triple Crown and went in to meet George Weiss, the Yankees general manager, expecting a big raise. To his astonishment Weiss said that he was going to cut Mantle's salary. In those days players did not have agents so Mantle was left to defend himself. When Mantle objected, Weiss pulled out a folder and said he had a private detective following Mantle for most of the season. "How would you like your wife to see this report?" he asked him. Mickey backed down and took the cut.

Mickey lived life to the fullest just like Ruth had around 30 years earlier. Mickey's father and two uncles had died of lung cancer at the age of 40 and Mickey was convinced he was going to die early. He later said that if he knew he was going to live as long he did he would have taken better care of himself.

In the summer of 1961, I went to New York to cover the two Yankees going after Ruth's record of 60 home runs in a season. One day Maris turned to Mantle and said, "Mick, I can't stand this, I can't stand all the pressure from the media." Mantle replied, "Well, you're just going to have to get used to it." Maris never really got used to the attention put on him that summer. One day Mickey gave the impression that play-ing baseball was not the biggest thing in his life—that he preferred to have fun. The photographer I was working with had a long lens attached to his camera. Mickey asked me if he could use the camera because there was a lady sitting in the centre field bleachers not wearing underpants. The photographer set it up and Mickey soon had the whole Yankee bench gathered around him.

I have a feeling that if it had been Mantle rather than Maris who broke the Babe's record, the fans would have accepted it. After all, Mantle was a real Yankee. Maris came to the Yankees after playing with Cleveland and Kansas City and never had a year like the one of 1961. New Yorkers are funny. Instead of hailing Maris, they turned on him. I was at the Yankee spring training camp in 1962 in Florida and when Maris stepped up to the plate he was booed by the Yankee faithful. Maris could never understand it and neither could I. Maris went to his grave a bitter man and was never voted into the Baseball Hall of Fame.

New York in the 1950s was the centre of the baseball universe. They had three teams and they all played in World Series. They also had three of the best centre fielders the game had ever seen: Mickey Mantle from the Yankees, Duke Snider from the Dodgers, and Willie Mays from the Giants. Mantle was not even the best of the three. That honour would have to go to Mays. Willie made his famous over-the-shoulder catch in the 1954 World Series as the Giants swept the Indians in four straight on the back of their star centre fielder.

I saw Mays play at the Polo Grounds against the St. Louis Cardinals and Stan Musial. But I did not get to talk to him until the Giants moved to San Francisco in 1958. Mays was the "Say Hey Kid" and the favourite of Leo Durocher, the crusty manager of the Giants. San Francisco, the city by the bay, may be one of the most beautiful in the country, but Mays never liked it as much as the Big Apple. Not that it affected his play. He wound up with 660 home runs and was at the time third on the all-time list.

For a time, Willie appeared destined to end up in the shadow of his godson Barry Bonds, who also plays for the Giants and had ambitions of overtaking Hank Aaron's home-run record. As it turns out, though, today's power hitter will likely never pass Aaron's record, much less overshadow Mays: Bonds is now plagued with a supposed knee injury and suspected steroid use.

Mays did return to New York to play for the Mets but was only a shadow of his former self. He was slow and could not hit like he once did. Unlike Williams he just did not know when to quit.

13

From the Elite to Defeat:
Baseball in Canada

ON CANADA DAY 2004, the Montreal Expos played the
Toronto Blue Jays in Puerto Rico: Canada's two teams meeting on our national holiday in a stadium in the Caribbean. It
is hard to believe that these teams, once among the elite in
baseball, have fallen so far. The Expos finally left Montreal
after the 2004 season, when they were lucky to draw 5,000
fans at home and were forced to play some of their games in
Puerto Rico. They are now reincarnated as the Washington
Nationals. Montreal was the first team to come to Canada,
and without the early success experienced in Montreal,
Toronto may have never gotten a team.

I was fortunate enough to be at Jarry Park in 1969 to
see the very first Expos game. They won that game over the
St. Louis Cardinals, and Montreal, once a hockey town,

began to embrace baseball. Jarry Park was really not much of a stadium but the fans did not really care because it was a fun place to watch baseball. Ron Fairly, who has the distinction of playing for both the Expos and the Blue Jays, compared Jarry Park to Fenway. When the Expos left the intimate surroundings of Jarry Park to move to the cavernous Olympic Stadium in 1977, they lost a lot of fan support. Olympic Stadium was never a good place to watch the game. But the Expos by then had a team that would soon be one of the best in baseball. They were going to be the team of the '80s capable of bringing the World Series to Canada for the very first time.

So where did they go wrong? Well, actually, the Expos should have gotten to the World Series in 1981. I covered their playoff games against the Dodgers in the 1981 postseason. The Expos came home leading the series three games to one. All they needed was a single win to move on.

The Dodgers, obviously not that confident, checked out of their hotel on the Saturday but to their shock won the next game. Sunday was rainy and overcast and the game was delayed. When the weather showed no signs of clearing, the game was postponed. Steve Rogers told me once that they could have played the game on Sunday when the rain had cleared, and he claimed that Charles Bronfman had prime minister Trudeau as his guest and assured the former Prime Minister that the game would not be played that day. So Trudeau headed back to Ottawa and when the weather cleared Bronfman refused to play the game and break his promise to Trudeau. Trudeau was blamed for a lot of things, so why not add this to the list?

The next day, still known as Black Monday in Montreal, turned out to be bright and cold. Rogers, the Expos ace starter, came out of the bullpen to pitch the ninth inning with the game still tied. Rick Monday hit a home run over the left field fence and sent the Dodgers to the World Series against the New York Yankees.

That Expos team had two players, Gary Carter and Andre Dawson, who were to win MVP awards but with other teams. The two Expos stars were never all that close. I was doing a magazine piece on Carter in the spring of 1982. Carter suggested that we go into the training room where he was seeking treatment. On the next table was Dawson. They never spoke to each other, which I found quite odd. I guess Dawson envied Carter's relationship with the media. Carter was never at a loss for a great story or a quote when you spoke to him.

No one was more heartbroken at the Expos loss than Bronfman, their multi-million dollar owner. He told me one day that he still hoped to bring a World Series to Montreal but unfortunately the Blue Jays beat him to the punch. Bronfman was the perfect owner; he hired good people to run the team then left them alone. His father, Sam, had built Seagrams into one of the most successful liquor companies in North America. The Expos were Charles's baby and he had free reign to run them as he saw fit. But even rich men find their patience if not their bankrolls can be exhausted. The Expos had been a team built from a great farm system, which produced a lot of their stars. But with free agency, a team, especially a team from Canada, could no longer hang on to their best players. Bronfman refused to get into the bidding wars and decided to sell the team and walk away from baseball and from his dream.

The team was taken over by a group headed by Claude Brochu, a former employee of Bronfman at the distillery. In the 1994 season the Expos had put together another great team due to their farm system. They had a record of 74 wins and 40 losses midway through the season. This was a team that included Larry Walker, a Canadian-born outfielder, and Pedro Martinez, a future Cy Young winner. This was the year that the rest of the season and the post-season were canceled due to a players' strike. By the time baseball resumed, the Expos could no longer afford to keep their star players. Walker went to Colorado where he won an MVP award, and Martinez went to the Boston Red Sox, where he became the most dominant pitcher in baseball.

The Expos had one last chance at consolidating themselves in Montreal. They had plans to build a new stadium but that never got off the ground. Major League Baseball became the owner of the Expos. This was after they were run into the ground by Jeffrey Loria, who left town to buy the Florida Marlins. The Expos, who once drew more than three million fans per season, were reduced to only drawing 5,000 fans a game in the cavernous Olympic Stadium.

The Expos have now been moved to Washington, D.C.—a sad ending to the team that brought baseball to Canada.

Major League Baseball finally came to Toronto in 1977. But it undoubtedly would have been here long before that, except there was no suitable stadium. Jack Cooke was going to buy the Washington Senators and move them to Toronto, but he was stopped in his tracks by his old rival John Bassett, the owner of the Toronto Argonauts, as well as the *Telegram* newspaper. He used his political input to stop Cooke from refurbishing the CNE Stadium for baseball. Ironically enough, it was the same plan used when the Blue Jays finally came to Toronto. In 1974 the Labatt brewing company had a deal to buy the San Francisco Giants and move them to Toronto. A group in San Francisco organized a campaign to keep the Giants. So Labatt decided to settle for an expansion team.

The Blue Jays actually got in on the coattails of the Seattle Mariners. The American League had moved the Seattle franchise, then known as the Pilots, to Milwaukee. But Seattle was in an uproar and threatened to sue Major League Baseball, so they put a team back in Seattle and Toronto came along, too, in order to balance out the American

League. Toronto was awarded an expansion franchise to start in the 1977 season.

There are a lot of people out there taking credit for bringing the Blue Jays to Toronto, including Paul Godfrey. Godfrey did convince Metro Council to invest $17.5 million into the refurbishing of Exhibition Stadium. I always thought the key man who brought baseball to Toronto was Don McDougall, the energetic head of Labatt. He figured that the team would be a good market for their beer, Labatt Blue. Labatt held a 60% interest in the team and the other 30% was held by R. Howard Webster, a Montreal financier. He was the silent partner in the group but very important, with his connections to big business in Canada. The CIBC held the other 10%, and for all of them it turned out to be a very profitable investment.

Toronto fell in love with its new baseball team almost from the start. The players were outnumbered by the city's media at the first spring training in Dunedin, a sleepy little Florida town where the Jays set up base and where they still are, 25 years later. The Jays played their very first regular season game against the Chicago White Sox at Exhibition Stadium. In typical Canadian fashion, it was played in a snowstorm and they had to clear the snow off the field before the game could begin. The game was a sellout, with 44,000 people showing up on that cold April day. The Jays won the game and Toronto discovered a new sports hero in Doug Ault, who hit two home runs in that first game. Doug, who passed away suddenly in

2004, would never again be great, but for that one day he was the toast of the town.

For the Jays, their first season was a little bumpy as they lost double as many games as they won. The best player on the team was the shortstop, Bob Bailor, the Jays' first pick in the expansion draft. But the player the fans embraced was Otto "the Swatto" Velez, the outfielder who early in the season was the leading hitter in the American League. He faded and so did the Jays as they finished the season 40 games below .500.

Peter Bavasi was the first president of the ball club and his slogan was "if you haven't got the steak, sell the sizzle." He did that effectively for the years he was around. It was Bavasi who put in place the people who were to run the team in their most successful years. Pat Gillick, a scout with the Yankees, was hired as the team's first general manager. Paul Beeston, an accountant, was actually the first person hired by the new club. The two were to team up and make the Jays one of the most successful franchises in baseball.

The Jays became the measuring stick for all other expansion teams. In 1985 they won their division, beating out the New York Yankees, on the second-last day of the regular season. They met the Kansas City Royals in the American League Championships for the right to go to the World Series. The Jays came home with a 3-1 lead in the series but, similar to what happened in Montreal years earlier, the Jays lost the last three games and the Royals went on to the World Series.

Chapter 13

The Jays may not have been ready for the series in 1985, but they sure should have been two years later. They had a two-game lead on the Detroit Tigers heading into the final weekend of the season. The Jays lost all three games to the Tigers, as their bats went silent. Their big slugger, George Bell, failed to get a hit in the series.

Bell, in 1987, was the first Blue Jay to win the American League Most Valuable Player award. He was a very temperamental man, who seemed to feel the world was against him. One day I walked into the clubhouse before an afternoon game and Bell started to scream at me. He was upset that the roof at the SkyDome had been left open. "They listen to you," Bell yelled, "and that's why the roof stayed open." I agree the fans do like the roof open, but I sure doubt that the Jays ever listened to me. When he came back to watch the 1991 All-Star Game in Toronto, he started to yell at me from the batting cage during batting practice. I never really knew what was bugging George, but then, few people did. George left Toronto for the Chicago White Sox, where his chief claim to fame was being traded for Sammy Sosa.

The first homegrown superstar of the Jays was Dave Stieb. He was an outfielder at Southern Illinois University, and the Jays turned him into a pitcher and a great one at that. He had half a dozen one-hitters when he finally came up with a no-hitter in 1990 against Cleveland. Stieb was a character both on and off the field. The media found him difficult to interview but I never really had any problems.

From the Elite to Defeat

"It takes one to know one" was the explanation of my colleague John Robertson at the *Toronto Sun*.

One of my favourite stories about Stieb was a complaint from fans about how he always adjusted his crotch. He decided he would solve the problem by not wearing his cup, which I described as the baseball version of Russian roulette. It's unfortunate that neither Stieb nor Bell, the big stars of the 1980s, were around when the team won a World Series. Stieb was on the roster but was only a benchwarmer on those championship teams.

You can make a pretty good case that if it had not been for the SkyDome the Jays would have never found the money to build their World Series teams. The man behind the Dome was Bill Davis, then the Ontario premier. It is said that Davis had a severe case of dome envy. Whatever the case, he decided Toronto needed a dome for their baseball and football franchises. The SkyDome, when completed, cost $600 million. It would have never been that expensive if it were not for the additions of the hotel and many other frills.

The Dome opened in 1989 to applause and with the fans in awe. The fans even stayed after the games just to watch the roof close. The Blue Jays also had a new manager. Jimy Williams was fired midway through the 1988 season and Cito Gaston was not the first choice for the job. Pat Gillick wanted Lou Piniella, but the Yankees wanted such a stiff price for him that the Jays gave up. They turned to Gaston, the hitting coach, and made him the new bench boss.

Chapter 13

Along with signing Gaston, the Blue Jays made several good moves that produced the best team in baseball. The big one was sending Fred McGriff and Tony Fernandez to San Diego for Roberto Alomar and Joe Carter. Carter was the big bat they needed to replace George Bell, while Alomar, in my opinion, was the greatest player to ever put on a Blue Jay uniform. Not only was he a great second baseman but he always came up with the key hit, including a home run that beat the Oakland A's in the 1992 American League Championship Series.

Gillick and Beeston were the perfect tandem. Beeston found the money and Gillick spent it. In the 1992 season Gillick signed Jack Morris, then one of the best pitchers in baseball, from the Minnesota Twins. Of course, it was not difficult to justify spending money as the Jays continued to play in front of 50,000 fans a game and were one of the most profitable teams in baseball.

The key to the Jays' success in the 1990s was their bullpen, with setup man Duane Ward and closer "Terminator" Tom Henke. The Jays played the Atlanta Braves managed by Bobby Cox in the 1992 World Series. Cox had been the manager of the Jays when they first became a power in the 1980s. The Jays won that series in six games. That Saturday night in Toronto, cars raced up and down Yonge Street tooting their horns. When the team returned home they received a massive welcome at a sold-out SkyDome.

It is an old adage in sports that winning the first time is easy and repeating is always very hard. Gillick did not sit on the championship roster. In 1993 he added all-star Dave Stewart from the Oakland A's and midway through the season added Rickey Henderson, also from the A's. After beating the Chicago White Sox in the ALCS, the Jays headed to Philadelphia to play the Phillies. This time the Jays were able to win it at home, on a home run by Joe Carter in the bottom of the ninth inning in game six. "Touch 'em all, Joe," Tom Cheek, the announcer for the Jays, yelled as Carter rounded the bases. It turned out to be the biggest hit in Blue Jay history and one of the biggest in World Series history.

I've always felt that Gaston never got the credit he deserved for managing back-to-back World Series winners. He was never named manager of the year and was never thought of again as an all-star manager. Cito did not make many mistakes in the years he managed the team.

The Jays never got the chance to win a third straight World Series. A strike halted the 1994 season and the series was cancelled. The Jays were not able to regain their fan base after the strike and there were some changes. Gillick left to go to the Seattle Mariners and his friend Gord Ash took over the team. The Jays signed Roger Clemens in 1996. The Rocket had two stellar years for the Jays, winning back-to-back Cy Young awards, but it did not pay off at the box office. The Jays' attendance was only slightly bigger when the Rocket pitched, compared with the other starters.

Chapter 13

Going to the Blue Jay games was no longer the in thing to do. Tickets were now easy to get and the team's attendance plummeted. The team that used to draw 50,000 a game was drawing 20,000.

The Jays are not on life support like their cousins in Montreal were but they need a winning team to have a hope of getting back their fans. Rogers has pumped more money into the payroll and refurbished the SkyDome, which is now known as the Rogers Centre. J.P. Ricciardi, the Jays general manager, sometimes acts as if he invented baseball, but he is certainly no Gillick in making the moves to build a new championship team. Only time will tell if this combination of cash and chutzpah will put a contending team on the field.

14

Covering Golf:
Palmer, Nicklaus, and Me

I WAS LUCKY ENOUGH to cover my first Masters Tournament in 1958 when Arnold Palmer won his first of four championships. I was also there in 1997 when Tiger Woods won the first of his four Masters. I have covered 10 U.S. Opens and six British Opens, but the Masters is still my favourite tournament.

Nothing really prepares you for the sheer beauty of the place. One day I was sitting at Amen Corner when a middle-aged man sat down beside me. We talked about Jack Nicklaus. When he got up and left, Tim Wharnsby, then a fellow journalist at the *Sun*, asked me if I knew who I'd been sitting beside. It was movie star Jack Nicholson and I had not even realized it.

There were a lot of things, though, that I did not like about the Masters. When I first went there, the only blacks in the place were the caddies and the waiters in the club-house. There were no black players or spectators. This was the way of life in the Deep South and Augusta National Golf Club, to their shame, went along with it. Charlie Sifford won the Los Angeles Open in 1958 played at Rivera, one of the great courses in the United States. But Augusta did not invite Sifford to the Masters despite his credentials.

Arnold Palmer, as everyone knows by now, won the 1955 Canadian Open at the Weston Golf Club in Toronto, his first professional golf win on tour. Sifford was the leader after the first day of that tournament. Palmer almost did not get into that Open. He had not filed his entry on time and the organizers decided when he appeared that he would not be allowed to play. Arnie was traveling in a trailer, a far cry from the private jet he later used. Tommy Bolt, a former U.S. Open champion, appealed to the organizers to let Palmer play. Palmer, who after all was the 1954 U.S. amateur champion, was then given permission to do so. The rest, of course, is history. One shot on the 4th hole in the final round showed us the kind of "go for broke style" that would be his trademark in later years. Arnie drove it into the woods on that hole and should have chipped out. That was the safe way that most golfers leading a tournament would have taken. But this was not Arnie's style of play. He hit a shot that somehow found its way through the woods to land on the green and made a birdie. He went on to win the championship.

I have one more personal memory of that tournament. In 1980, Arnie came back to Weston on the 25th anniversary of his win. They had a putting contest for the media and believe it or not I won the damn thing. I have an autographed copy of one of Palmer's books, which he inscribed to "Jim, what a putter!"

The Masters was Palmer's stage. He won when television was first becoming a big deal. You can make the case that Palmer and TV together dragged golf into the big time. In 1959, at my second Masters, Palmer went into the final round tied with Stan Leonard of Vancouver. Leonard worked as a club pro in his early years and it was not until he was well into his 30s that he finally had the chance to play on the PGA tour. On the final day of that tournament, the weather had turned chilly at least by Augusta's standards. I showed up at the course in a short-sleeved golf shirt and Leonard spotted me and called me over.

"You look cold," he said, and grabbed a jacket out of his golf bag and tossed it to me.

I can't imagine any of the modern golfers doing the same thing. But it was a different era.

Neither Leonard nor Palmer won that tournament. The eventual champion was Art Wall, who overtook both of them on the final nine holes. Leonard's partner, Cary Middlecoff, was a notoriously slow player. Leonard was bothered, as anyone would be, by his deliberate play. After the tournament, Clifford Roberts, the imperious chairman of the Augusta National, wrote a letter to Leonard apologizing for pairing him with Middlecoff. I don't know whether Leonard, if he had been paired with Palmer, which he should have been, would have won the tournament. But it certainly would have improved his chances.

Palmer was to win four Masters Tournaments on a golf course he owned. In those days the champion played a round on the Monday after the tournament with Dwight Eisenhower, then president of the United States. You can say that while Palmer walked the fairways with presidents and kings, he never lost the common touch.

I still think Palmer hung on too long. It was painful to watch this once-great champion struggle to break 80. There was one time during those years that I was not so sure he should quit. Dead last after the first round, Palmer played on the Friday by himself with a marker. I followed him on the back nine that day and it was just like the good old days. Every time Arnold made a good shot, the fans gave him a standing ovation. They loved Arnie and he loved the galleries, who appreciated him at Augusta as at no other tournament.

I was at the 1989 PGA in Kemper Lakes near Chicago when Palmer made his last serious charge at the only major tournament he had never won. On the final day of that tournament, a scorching day in Chicago with the temperature in the 90s, Palmer wore a straw hat, but as the TV cameras zoomed in for coverage, he took it off and played bare-headed just like in the good old days when he was the king. I was also at the U.S. Open at Oakmont, Pennsylvania in 1994 when

Palmer made his final appearance. This was a course where Jack Nicklaus had beaten Palmer to win his first U.S. Open. The fans never forgave Nicklaus for beating their hero on a course just a few miles from Palmer's home in Latrobe.

I was also at the 1995 British Open at St. Andrews when Palmer made his final appearance in a tournament he had won twice. Needless to say, he got a standing ovation as he crossed the Swilken Bridge on his way to the 18th green. I found it interesting that Nicklaus, playing two groups ahead of Palmer, did not stay around to watch Arnie finish. Nick Faldo stayed to join in the applause as Palmer walked off the historic course for the final time.

Nicklaus, of course, eclipsed Palmer as the greatest golfer of all time. Tiger Woods may some day pass him, too, but I wouldn't hold my breath. Someone once said to Arnie, "Nicklaus may be the better player but they still love you, Arnie." Nothing could be more fitting for the most exciting player any of us is likely to see.

The ways Arnie and Jack managed to quit smoking says a lot about the difference between the two golfers. Palmer, who chain-smoked during the early years of his career, was told by his doctors that he should quit. Like most smokers, Palmer went through the torments of the damned before he finally beat the habit. Nicklaus told me one day at Augusta that he, too, had quit smoking. "I was driving back to my house in Palm Beach when I decided I should quit," Nicklaus said. "I threw my pack of cigarettes out the car window and never smoked again."

It was that amazing willpower that had as much as anything to do as Jack's amazing ability to do whatever he wanted on the golf course. Sure he could hit the ball a mile and put the lights out. As the legendary Bobby Jones once said, "He plays a game of which I am not familiar."

I first interviewed Nicklaus in the spring of 1962, the year he had won the first of his four U.S. Opens. Nicklaus was a pudgy young man who had the nickname Fat Jack. He told me he could never understand why the golf fans wouldn't accept him. Later he realized they never forgave him for beating their icon on so many occasions. The same thing happened to Roger Maris when he beat Mickey Mantle and broke Babe Ruth's record of 60 homers in a season.

Nicklaus won four U.S. Opens and six Masters but it was not really until his final Masters win in 1986 that he gained the acceptance of the older generation of golf fans. Of all the Masters I have covered, and there have been a lot of great ones, that was the best one on my list. That was the day that Jack turned back the clock and at the age of 46 became the oldest champion in the history of the event. He made a lot of key shots that day. The one I won't forget is the putt he sank on the 16th hole. It seemed that he almost willed that ball into the hole. I'm not so sure he didn't. As Jack walked up the

18th fairway with his son, Jackie, who was caddying for him, there was not a dry eye in the house. It was his son who told his father he still had a chance even with a five-shot difference between him and the leader on the final day. Nicklaus was never able to achieve that level of greatness again. But no one at his age had ever done it and anyone who was there would agree that Jack was one of the greatest.

Nicklaus has a special relationship with Canadian golf. He designed Glen Abbey in Oakville, Ontario, the home of so many Canadian Opens and the first course he designed on his own. It was a course ahead of its time as it provided excellent vantage points for spectators to see lots of thrilling golf. It also had a great finishing hole, as Tiger Woods proved when he hit a 6 iron out of a bunker that landed inches from the hole, on his way to winning the 2000 Canadian Open.

Our Open was one of the few major tournaments that Nicklaus never won. He was second no less than five times, once losing in a playoff to Tom Weisskopf at Royal Montreal. I once asked Nicklaus if he was going to keep playing in the Canadian Open.

"Sure I am," he said. "I'll keep playing 'til I get it right."

Unfortunately, time ran out on Jack and he never won it.

If the Masters was Palmer's stage, the U.S. Open belonged to Ben Hogan. He won it four times, the last three after a car accident that nearly took his life. Doctors warned Hogan that he would be lucky to walk again, let alone play golf. But they underestimated the willpower of this remarkable man. Few golfers, except for Tiger Woods in 2000, have ever had a year like Hogan did in 1953. He won the Masters and the U.S. Open by a margin of four shots. In those days they played 36 holes on the final day and it was a struggle for Hogan to walk let alone play golf.

The British Open that year was played at Carnoustie, and for the first time Hogan decided to enter. He won, to take the first three majors of the professional Grand Slam. Hogan never got a chance to complete it because he declined to play in the PGA Championships, for a lot of reasons. He arrived home from Scotland to a tickertape parade in New York and he felt he did not have enough time to get his game in shape for the PGA. Back then, the PGA was match play and Hogan just wasn't up for playing two 18-hole matches in a single day.

The British Open win was the last major that Hogan ever won. He did come close to other wins on a couple of occasions. In 1955 he lost a U.S. Open in San Francisco in a playoff to Jack Fleck, a club pro from Iowa. It was Hogan's putting that finally did him in. I recall watching him play the 16th hole in the final round of the 1956 Open in Rochester. Hogan stood over a two-foot putt for what seemed an eternity. He just could not control his hands, which were shaking erratically. He missed the putt and lost the tournament by one shot. Cary Middlecoff was the winner.

Hogan, unlike his rival, Sam Snead, was not a very approachable man, but he did establish in 1951 the Champions Dinner at the Masters. The tradition that the defending champion not only buys dinner for the other former champions, but also chooses the menu, is now a fixture of the Masters weekend.

In the 1960s, Hogan and Snead played together in the final round of the Masters. Hogan shot a 66 that day and Snead a 67. Later in the locker room the two old rivals were reminiscing. Both at the time were 48.

"Ben, in two years we can play on the Senior Tour," said Snead.

"Sam, you can play it, but if I can't play with these guys, I won't play," replied Hogan, and he never did.

It's hard to imagine two golfers less alike than Hogan and Snead. Hogan seldom spoke, and certainly not on the golf course. Snead loved to talk and his stories were the highlights of the Champions Dinner as long as he lived. Hogan, of course, owned the U.S. Open, and Snead never won it. Sam blew away a five-shot lead in the final round one year and that was the first of many U.S. Open disasters for him.

Snead was an amazing physical specimen. I was in the locker room between rounds at the 1961 U.S. Open, when Snead was holding out his hand at shoulder height and testing his flexibility by kicking his hand. This was a feat for a gymnast, let alone a man closing in on 50. Sam lived life to the fullest. He was never one to leave a party early and when he did leave it was often on the arm of a young lady. Sam was enticed to play in the Canadian Open with promises of a fishing trip with a pretty young female.

Sometimes his high living caught up with him. He was arrested for driving under the influence when traveling to the Champions Dinner one day in the '80s. But he talked his way out of it and that night sat at the head table.

Sam had a hundred stories and some of them may have been true. One day, when he was in Toronto playing a seniors event, he told me about a wartime tournament. Sam claimed that at the Los Angeles Open, Bing Crosby had given him a Spalding Dot, then the favourite ball on the tour and hard to get. Snead said, "I used the ball for all 72 holes and won the tournament."

Until Mike Weir came along, a Canadian had never won a Masters. Stan Leonard gave it a shot, but George Knudson in 1969 came the closest. Knudson lost that year to George Archer, and there was no comparison between the two golfers. The Canadian outplayed the eventual winner handily, except for on the greens. As with many Canadian golfers, putting was the weakness in Knudson's game. I often felt that George was not really into putting, but was a masterful striker of the ball. He was often compared to Hogan as a shotmaker, but on the greens it was another matter.

Knudson once told me he went to Las Vegas and played blackjack at $1,000 a hand because he felt it might steel his nerves when he stood over a crucial putt. But we'll never know whether it ever paid off. As long as he lived, George was a man who enjoyed every minute of his life. I was at Doral in Florida in the 1960s and hooked up with Knudson in the bar. He was then drinking Scotch mists, a potent drink that put me under the table after only two. When I staggered out of the bar, Knudson was still there. The next day on the Blue Monster, a course at Doral, he shot a 68. He was also a chain-smoker, as so many people were in that era. He developed lung cancer and died on January 24, 1989, just 51 years old. I wrote in my column in the *Sun* the day after his death that it was too bad he did not win the Masters because no one would have enjoyed the Champions Dinner more than he would have.

Anytime I recall some of the great golfers I've known, Lee Trevino is near the top of the list. Trevino feared no one on the golf course, even the Golden Bear Nicklaus. In 1971 he became the first golfer to win the U.S., British, and Canadian Opens. Trevino also won the PGA in 1974, and the only major that eluded him during his career was the Masters. He declined to play at Augusta for many years because he objected to the way the club treated minorities. When he did show up, he would change his golf shoes in the parking lot and go directly to the first tee. He refused to go into the Augusta National Clubhouse.

Trevino had come to golf the hard way. He hustled to make a buck on the municipal courses in Texas. Once he was asked if he felt the pressure in a major championship.

"Hell, no," Trevino replied. "Pressure is playing a Nassau with only $5 in your pocket."

Trevino was never at a loss for words. His non-stop talking on the course was not popular among his competitors, but he did not care. He was playing in the British Open at Muirfield when he was asked if he remembered the tournament where he had beaten Nicklaus.

"That was 20 years and three wives ago," Trevino said.

For reasons I don't quite understand, all of his wives have been name Claudia.

"It saves getting the towels embroidered again," Trevino explained.

That same year at Muirfield he was asked about Bernhard Langer, a notoriously slow player.

"I wouldn't say he was slow," Trevino said. "But when he teed off on the first hole he was clean shaven and when he got to the ninth hole he had a full grown beard."

Trevino may not rank with Nicklaus and Palmer but he is not that far behind.

Greg Norman is without a doubt the best golfer never to win the Masters, but he certainly had his chances. In 1987 he lost in a playoff to Larry Mize, the young man who grew up in Augusta and used to operate the scoreboard during previous Masters tournaments. That year, Norman went into a playoff with Mize and Seve Ballesteros. Seve went out on the first extra hole. On the second extra hole Mize hit a chip from 40 feet off the green that somehow found the bottom of the cup for a birdie. Norman missed his difficult birdie putt and Mize walked away the Masters champion. Norman said later that it was the most devastating loss of his career.

Unfortunately, worse was yet to come. The 1996 Masters convinced a lot of observers and perhaps Norman that he was destined never to win the tournament. He entered the final round that year with a six-shot lead over playing partner Nick Faldo. There seemed no way Norman could lose except the way he did. By the time they finished nine holes, Faldo had cut Norman's lead in half. But Greg had owned the back nine during the previous rounds and it seemed this would be no different.

I followed Norman that day and I found it painful to watch the greatest collapse in major championship history. No one had ever lost a major going into the final round with a six-shot lead. As they walked up the 18 fairway, Norman appeared a defeated man. Faldo did not play spectacular golf but his 67 was good enough to beat Norman's 78. Even Faldo looked as if he felt sorry for Norman as they embraced on the 18 green.

Chapter 14

As it happened it was April 14, the anniversary of the sinking of the Titanic, something I was to note in a *Toronto Sun* column. Norman got over the loss philosophically.

"The sun will get up tomorrow," he said.

But you could tell he was deeply hurt.

The only majors that Norman ever won were the British Open, not that great a record for a man of his talent. In 1986 Norman was the 54-hole leader in all four of the major championships. The only one he won was the British Open.

Moe Norman shares the same surname as the Australian superstar. He should have been a great player on the PGA tour. Lee Trevino once said that Moe was the best ball striker he had seen since Ben Hogan.

There are a lot of reasons that Moe never realized his potential. He was painfully shy, so much so that he hid in the caddie shack at the Ontario Open instead of going to accept the trophy he had won.

Moe was invited to the Masters in the 1960s as the Canadian amateur champion but he spent so much time on the practice tee he blistered his hands and was hardly able to hold a club the next day.

He was an eccentric, which I always felt was due to his shyness. He had a running battle with the Royal Canadian Golf Association when he was an amateur because he used to sell the prizes he won in the tournaments. He was so sure of winning that he sold them before he even teed off. I spoke to Moe's father about the selling of the prizes.

"What did they expect him to do, rent a warehouse?" he said.

One year at the Canadian Open in his home town of Kitchener, Norman was within two shots of the lead after the third round. I raced after him to try to get an interview as he ran down the driveway of the Westmount course.

"Can't wait, can't wait, I have to get to Rockaway." he said. "I've got a couple of marks on a ten buck bet."

In the 1960s, he was giving golf lessons on a driving range on the outskirts of Toronto. Milt Dunnell, my boss at the *Star*, said I might get a story if I took a lesson from him. I stepped on to the tee box and Moe told me to hit a couple. After that he took the club from my hand and for the rest of the lesson he hit balls. Perhaps Moe was smarter than I thought because he knew not even a lesson could help my golf game. He had an amazing memory and was close to being a genius at mathematics.

Moe had open heart surgery in London, Ontario in the 1980s. When he woke up after the anesthetic wore off, doctors asked him if he knew where he was.

"On the 4th hole at the Hunt Club," he replied.

The hospital was built on the grounds of the University of Western Ontario where the old London Hunt Club used to be.

Chapter 14

It wasn't 'til later in life that he achieved a bit of financial success. His video on the golf swing became a bestseller. He had a contract with Titleist to provide him with 10 dozen golf balls a year. Back then, Moe used to winter in Florida and drove in his Cadillac almost every day to Royal Oak, a course near the Kennedy Space Center. I went there for several years for a winter golfing holiday and every day Moe could be seen looking for golf balls off the first tee. He liked playing with the balls he found so he could sell the ones Titleist gave him.

Moe, who died in September 2004, was one of a kind, and I doubt we will ever see his like again.

The most accomplished Canadian golfer of all time is not Knudson, Leonard, Norman, or even Mike Weir. It has to be Marlene Stewart Streit, the first and only Canadian to be elected to the World Golf Hall of Fame in St. Augustine, Florida. Marlene, as she closes in on 70, is still winning tournaments. She captured all major tournaments she entered but never turned pro. If she had I think she would have dominated the LPGA tour like no one else.

I have a special reason for speaking kindly of Marlene. The first sports story I ever wrote for the *Toronto Daily Star* in 1951 was on Marlene. She was then a 17-year-old schoolgirl who defeated Ada McKenzie at the Ontario Ladies'

Championship at Toronto's Lambton Golf & Country Club. The story appeared on page one of the next day's paper. It was the first of many stories I wrote about Marlene and there was a good chance anytime you covered a tournament she was playing in that your story would end up on the front page.

A friend of mine once asked me how anyone who could write as well about golf as I did could play so badly. I took it as a compliment. My father was a good enough golfer to qualify to play in the U.S. Amateur. He once held a course record of 63 at the Sarnia Golf Club, a record that was broken by Sam Snead.

Every golfer has a day when everything seems to be working on the course. As golfers like to say, you're in the zone. Mine came in the late 1950s at Oakland Hills in Detroit; this was the site of the 2004 Rider Cup and a course Hogan called "the monster" the year he won the 1951 U.S. Open there.

That day I played the first four holes in two shots under par. I holed a 3 wood for a birdie and knocked in a 5 iron for another. I even made a routine par by blasting out of a sand trap. You will have to take my word for it, since my playing partners have all moved on to the big golf course in the sky. If I had it to do it over again I should have quit after four holes and walked off muttering, "This course isn't tough enough for a golfer of my calibre."

I finished the round and despite the start just barely broke 100. I have played some of the great golf courses of the world and even hit a few decent shots, but never again have I had a round like that one over 40 years ago in Detroit. I somehow doubt I ever will.

15

Media Scrum:

Working with Dunnell, Gross, Beddoes, et al.

I'VE BEEN LUCKY ENOUGH to work with and against some of the great names in journalism. When I was in university, I picked up *The Globe and Mail* every morning just to read Jim Coleman. He was one of the most amusing journalists this country has ever produced. I've spent a good long time with Coleman and I even consider him a good friend. When I got a column in the *Sun* in 1983, later in my career, I got a call from Coleman offering advice.

"Just don't screw up," he told me.

I was also fortunate enough to work for Milt Dunnell, sports editor of the *Toronto Star*. When he was in charge, from 1948 to 1970, the *Star* had the best sports pages in Canada. One of the big reasons was Dunnell's column. He wrote well on every sport but especially loved horse racing and hockey. Milt was at Churchill Downs in 1964 when Northern Dancer took the race and received the roses. Reading his column 40 years later you can still catch that magical moment.

Some of Dunnell's finest writing was about boxing. He covered the fight in Zaire between Muhammad Ali and George Foreman. Most of the great sportswriters at the time were there, but no one did it better than Dunnell. He was known and respected throughout the business. Wherever you were, other writers would tell you to give their regards to Milt.

Milt came to the sports department from the newsroom where he was assistant city editor. As a result of this background, he knew a good story and how to get it. Milt was respected not only by his peers in the business, but by publishers of rival papers. John Bassett, the publisher of the *Telegram*, also owned the Argonauts. He used to drive other writers crazy by leaking stories to Dunnell. If you really wanted to know what was going on with the Argos you would have to read his column.

If there was one criticism of Dunnell it was that he seldom used his column to be really critical, but when he did, he went all out, and people definitely took notice. He did step out of character when he appeared on the *Sports Hot Seat* television program on CTV.

Once on *Sports Hot Seat*, Milt teed off on Muhammed Ali and a rock was thrown through the window of his house by an irate viewer. Milt never had to worry about readers of the *Star* taking the law into their own hands, but television exposes you to a lot of kooks.

Milt was a delight to work for. If you did your job, you would seldom hear from him. He would also provide his staff with exciting work. He sent me to the Masters in 1958, the first time a Canadian reporter had ever been to an Augusta National. Milt also sent me to cover the suspension of Rocket Richard in 1955 and the riots that were to come. I was the only one representing a Toronto paper at that event. Later that year I was sent to Vancouver for the annual meeting of the Canadian Football League. I was able to break the story of the Grey Cup's move to Vancouver for the 1955 season.

Milt continued to write his column well into his 80s. The *Star* wanted him to continue but he decided to pack up his typewriter in the 1990s. I called Milt on Christmas Eve 2004 as I was working on this book to wish him a happy 99th birthday.

It's a tribute to Dunnell that many have tried but no one has yet to replace him as head columnist of the *Star*. The closest was the late Jim Proudfoot, who shared Dunnell's love for racing and hockey.

Proudfoot was not only an entertaining writer but a great travel connoisseur. He loved good food and good wine. Once, during a Super Bowl in San Francisco, my wife, Caroline, and

Chapter 15

I accompanied him to dinner. My share of the cheque ate up my per diem for the week, but it was worth it.

Proudfoot died in 2001 at the age of 67, long before his time. I'll miss him and so will the readers of the *Star*.

I also worked for George Gross at the *Toronto Sun*, which was indeed an interesting experience. George escaped from Czechoslovakia, according to legend, by swimming the Danube. He came to Canada in 1950 and worked on a farm. At the time he was fluent in five languages but English was not one of them.

George finally landed at the *Toronto Telegram* to cover soccer. It was not a major sport or a major beat but Gross made it bigger than it was. George also covered figure skating, the preferred sport of Lady Eaton, whose husband was a major shareholder in the *Telegram*.

At the 1976 Winter Olympics in Innsbruck, Austria, most of the other media lived in the dorms of the university. It was good enough for the *New York Times*, the *Chicago Tribune*, *The Globe and Mail*, but Gross, at great expense to the *Sun*, stayed at the Holiday Inn located in the heart of the city. Only one Canadian medal came out of those games but I'm sure Gross still enjoyed himself.

Gross is one of the best-dressed sportswriters in the business. You would seldom see him without a shirt and tie.

He celebrated his 80th birthday in 2003 and still writes his weekly column for the *Sun*, which he joined in 1971, and has no intention of giving it up.

If I was asked to pick the most influential member of the sports media in my lifetime, there is not much doubt it would be Foster Hewitt, the hockey broadcaster. Twenty years after Foster's death, Bob Cole from *Hockey Night in Canada* still covers the game the way Foster did. It is a radio broadcast with pictures because that's the way Hewitt did it and Cole saw no reason to change.

Foster got into radio almost by accident. His father, W.A. Hewitt, was sports editor of the *Star*. The *Star* had one of the first radio stations in Toronto and Foster was assigned by his father to broadcast the games. Though he had no experience in broadcasting, he proved to be a natural.

When the Leafs traveled to the west coast, Hewitt was almost as big a name to the locals as any of the players. He made hockey live for millions of Canadians from St. John's to Vancouver.

In 1972 CTV was to broadcast the Summit Series and hired Foster to do the play-by-play. There was really no other choice because at the time he was the voice of hockey. Foster's call of "Henderson scores for Canada" caught the drama of that final game.

Chapter 15

Foster, a wealthy man, was very careful with the dollar. He was often slow to pick up a cheque. He was unpredictable, though. Once a bunch of us were drinking at a bar in the Plaza Hotel in Boston. The group included Leaf coach Punch Imlach, who seldom let a cheque go by. When it was time to pay, Imlach asked for the cheque and was informed that Foster, who had already left the table, had picked it up. I guess you could say Foster beat him to the punch.

In 1952 when they first started to televise Leaf games, Conn Smythe, owner of the team, was not convinced that the new medium was here to stay. So it was decided that Foster was to do the same broadcast for both radio and TV. Now, more than 50 years later, nothing has changed.

Dick Beddoes, like Ralph Allen, Jim Coleman, and Scott Young before him, came out of the west to write a sports column for *The Globe and Mail*. Beddoes had established his reputation as an outspoken columnist for the *Vancouver Sun* and no one ever had any doubt about where he stood on an issue. He was the Don Cherry of his time, as famous for his outlandish dress as for his writing. His favourite garb was a cape with a hat to match.

In 1972 the *Globe*, for reasons that escape me, decided not to send Beddoes to Moscow. Dick decided to go on his own and worked freelance for a couple of Canadian radio stations. He was besieged by fans from across Canada for his autograph. He wrote a book on that series but it was never published. When he left the *Globe*, Beddoes turned to television. No one at the time did it with more flare than he. I was a frequent guest on his program. He would pick me up in a chauffeur-driven limo to take me to the studio in Hamilton. I was not impressed when the limo pulled up in front of my house, but my children certainly were.

Beddoes, who died from cancer in 1988, was one of a kind. He is missed not only by colleagues in the media but by sports fans across the country.

One of the true characters in the sports writing business was Ted Reeve, who toiled for the *Toronto Telegram* and later the *Sun*. Ted had been a great athlete in his time, blocking a punt in the 1928 Grey Cup game. He also coached the Queen's University team and later the Montreal team in the old Big Four.

Ted never got past high school but still was one of the best-read people I have known. He also had a great sense of humour. He was once called in Montreal by a man who asked when that afternoon's game would start. Ted replied, "When do you want us to start?"

My family spent many winters with the Reeves at Vero Beach, Florida. Ted used to write his columns before they left Toronto and then mailed them back to the paper when he got

Chapter 15

to Vero Beach. Once he showed me a column he had written in Toronto on the Chicago Cubs training camp.

"Ted," I told him, "the Cubs play in Arizona."

He replied, "They won't know any better."

He was right. They ran the column.

The Reeves' home at the beach was a favourite gathering place with his friends, where he held court every morning. He invited me up once for a cup of coffee. But the coffee turned out to be rum with a bit of coffee mixed in.

Ted was into his 90s when he died. Some of the mourners at his funeral were the lieutenant governor, the premier and most of his cabinet, the mayor, and the bartender of the press club. I doubt if we'll ever see a character like Reeve in the sportswriting fraternity again.

The big change in media in my lifetime has been the arrival of television. It's the TV commentators who announce the big stars. The most prominent of them in Canada is the CBC's Brian Williams. I never realized how famous Brian was, until he showed up to visit me in the hospital when I was recovering from knee surgery. There was a buzz up and down the halls and the nurses were very impressed that I knew Brian Williams.

Brian and I go way back to the early days of Citytv. Even then you knew he had a real talent for the medium. One day after the show, Moses Znaimer, who founded the station, came up to Brian and told him that he belonged in television.

No one works any harder than Williams to provide a telecast. But I think what endears him to viewers is his enthusiasm for the events he covers. He brings events at Olympic Games alive so that you feel that you are there. One of his best broadcasts was the 100 meter final in Seoul, when Ben Johnson won the gold medal in world-record time. When Ben was stripped of his medal for using drugs, Brian was as chagrined as any of us. But it did not stop him from covering one of the most shameful events in Canadian sports.

Newspaper columnists have decided that there is no point in trying to compete with TV, so they might as well join in. Sports writers who find they can add to their bank roll by appearing on the blue screen include Stephen Brunt of *The Globe and Mail* and Steve Simmons of the *Sun*. They both appear frequently on television and radio as well as atop their columns in their newspapers.

Sometimes it seems that every time you turn on your TV set there is Brunt. Brunt graduated from the University of Western Ontario, in music. His dad was a jazz musician and he wanted to follow in his footsteps. He became a music reviewer for the *Globe* and wound up in the sports department almost by accident.

Chapter 15

Brunt is an exception to the rule that you have to write hockey to be a successful sports columnist in this country. Hockey is one of his least favourite sports and he hardly ever writes about it. His favourite sport is boxing and he has written several books on the matter. One of his best includes a series of interviews of men who had lost to the great Muhammad Ali.

No one in the business is more versatile than Brunt. He has also written documentaries for the National Film Board on boxing. Brunt and I agree on one thing: We both have a soft spot in our hearts for the CFL. One event he and I will never miss is the Grey Cup game.

The *Toronto Sun*'s Steve Simmons is a journalism graduate of Western. He worked at the *Calgary Herald* and co-authored a book with Lanny McDonald. But Steve always wanted to be a columnist in his hometown—Toronto. He finally made it and in most ways is very different than Brunt. Simmons thrives on controversy and never misses a chance to take a shot at an athlete, coach, or manager. His best sport is hockey, a game he understands better than most and writes about better than anyone I have known.

Simmons has carved out a career in both television and radio. He and Brunt both rely on their personalities and opinions to carry them when on screen.

The sports media have changed dramatically over the 50 years I have spent in the trade. The newspaper columnists were once the top dogs. They have had to take a back seat to the electronic media. But Brunt and Simmons bring something to the table that TV and radio personalities always lack, and as long as they do the future of print journalism is a bright one.

When I was growing up in Sarnia, the biggest star was Tom Harmon, halfback of the Michigan Wolverines. In one game he scored all 30 points for Michigan. In addition to playing halfback he also was the kicker, the punter, and a member of the defence.

It was one of the highlights of my career when I met this great man at the 1976 Winter Olympic Games. He was there for ABC Radio. He did not know how to send his material and I showed him how to hook up a tape recorder to the telephone, just about the only technical skill I have mastered. As a youngster I would have wet my pants meeting my sports hero. But you never know what will happen in your lifetime.

You run into a lot of the jerks in this business, especially people in television, whose egos are often bigger than their talents. There is no doubt that the biggest jerk I've ever met is Howard Cosell.

Chapter 15

You can excuse some people for being full of themselves after reaching fame. But Howard was not one of them. I met Howard in the early days before he reached ABC's *Wide World of Sports*. One day Cosell showed up late for a New York Rangers press conference. By the time he got there it was long over and Howard decided to make a scene.

"Do you know who I am?" he yelled at the Rangers PR man.

You have to admit, few people in television made the impact Cosell did. He made Monday night football and did it so well. Half the audience of the program hated him but they tuned in anyways. Howard made his career, though, by broadcasting the great fights of Muhammad Ali. Ali always claimed he made Cosell and Cosell of course claimed it was the other way around. Howard was objectionable on the air and that was a good part of his appeal on and off the air.

In my lifetime nothing has done more to change the way people follow sports than television. We now can sit in our living rooms and watch sporting events from all over the world. We actually take it for granted. It wasn't always so easy, at least not for those of us doing the broadcasting.

The first Summer Olympics I covered, for the *Star Weekly*, were the 1964 games in Tokyo, Japan. CBC had to fly the film to Hawaii and transmit it from there to Canada. The viewers ended up watching day-old events. One of the greatest events I covered was the 1954 Empire Games in Vancouver. If not for the Summit Series in 1972 it would have been the best of the lot. It matched Australia's John Landy and England's Roger Bannister, at the time the only two men to ever run a four-minute mile.

The Empire Games in Vancouver was the first time Landy and Bannister had shared the same track. Landy took the lead and held it till they reached the stretch, then Bannister turned on the jets and passed him. There is a famous picture of Landy looking over his shoulder, watching his opponent gaining on him. One of the secrets of the race is that John Landy had stepped on a photographer's flash bulb before the race, cutting his foot. Landy said nothing about it, not wanting to use the injury as an excuse if he were to lose the race.

So how did Canadians watch this event? It went from Seattle to New York, then back to Toronto.

The 1952 Grey Cup game between Toronto and Edmonton was the first to be televised. It was only shown live in the east. They had to fly the film out to Winnipeg, where it was broadcast to the west the following day.

Hockey made its debut in the same year. It wasn't considered a big deal. The broadcast started in the second period and it was more than a decade later when they finally decided to carry a complete game.

The NFL is the most successful sports enterprise at using television for profit. All franchises receive the same amount of TV money, so the Green Bay Packers in the smallest market receive the same as the New York Giants, the team in the biggest market. At the time, the owners did not think it was that big a deal so they agreed to split the revenue. Nothing has made the NFL such a competitive league more than this policy. The Green Bay Packers have won championships and so have the New York Giants. Some of the big market teams like the Detroit Lions have yet to win in the Super Bowl era.

There has always been an argument that live TV can hurt the gate. The NFL has a blackout policy, where if the game is not sold out by the Thursday, the game will not be broadcast in the home city. The Blue Jays in their glory years never blacked out one game. That, of course, was a time when the Blue Jays were selling out SkyDome with crowds of 50,000. Now that attendance has dropped to 20,000, they may have to re-examine the policy.

You have to wonder how long it will be before teams start charging for TV games. They already are showing some hockey games on pay-per-view in Vancouver and Calgary. It's a source of revenue that the owners will be hard pressed to pass up.

In the 1960s, when many of the Leaf games were not on television, they decided to show them at theatres in Toronto. It was not a success, so pay-per-view was abolished after a one-year trial. I'm sure the current owners of the Leafs, who have their own TV network, will eventually provide games for a fee. It is only a question of time because the money is there for the taking.

Television has become so much a part of our culture that sports not on TV are the sports that don't really matter. In the 1970s the CFL used to black out games. It is claimed that it resulted in the loss of a whole generation of fans. When the Canadian game was not on TV, viewers turned to the NFL and many of them never returned. The truth of the matter is that television, at least for football, is a better way to watch it. Instant replay, some of it in slow motion, gives an appreciation of the game you don't get when it's live.

Hockey has never been a success as a TV sport. That is one reason it has not made it on American networks. But in the future I expect television will find a way to transfer the speed and toughness of hockey to the screen.

What will be the next electronic medium for sports? Will it be the Internet? Already you can sit at your computer and pick up radio broadcasts from sports events all over the world. No longer do you have to wait for the morning newspaper to get the scores. They are available on the Net. The addition of fantasy sports may have a lot to do with the revival of baseball. Fans can sit at home with their computers and become a George Steinbrenner. The NFL is also very popular in the fantasy sports world. It's the one big reason people pay for services, such as NFL Sunday Ticket, that provide coverage of all the games across the United States.

Chapter 15

I've learned not only to live with but to enjoy television. But I still wonder if young people today are missing out on the excitement of a radio broadcast. I grew up listening to Foster Hewitt's description of Leaf games on radio. I remember the first time I came to Maple Leaf Gardens to see a game live. My first impression was that they were skating too slow. Certainly not at the breathtaking speed they were in Foster's broadcast.

Growing up in Sarnia I never dreamed I'd live to see the day when I could watch sports events from the four corners of the world. I wonder what another generation will think of the new and different ways networks will develop to cover major sporting events. I'm sure it will be something special.

The biggest change in TV has been the 24-hour sports networks—ESPN in the U.S. and TSN in Canada. No one ever thought you could justify a 24-hour sports network, including me. We were all proven wrong. Now, 25 years later, ESPN is still on the air and has been one of the great successes in television history. Tracy McGrady, a basketball star with the Toronto Raptors, quit the team and gave the reason that he could not watch highlights of himself on the Canadian network. I guess TSN did not satisfy him and he objected to all that curling and hockey.

The man who put TSN on the air was Gordon Craig, a former CBC producer. I worked with Craig and the late Jim Thompson at the 1967 Pan American Games in Winnipeg. I was the chief writer and I got a lot of help from veteran producers like Craig and managed to blunder through. Thompson left TSN to become president of the Canadian Olympic Federation. He later died prematurely of a heart attack and never really got the chance to turn around the Olympic program. You could make the case that Craig is the most important Canadian media executive in this age of television.

Television still features in my life. I continue to guest on *Sportsnet* and Fan 590 radio's program *Prime Time Sports.* I'm keeping my hand in the print medium, too, by writing a weekly column for the *Toronto Sun*. I suppose it makes sense that I would continue doing a bit of work in my retirement years. However, as the title of this book indicates, the terms "work" and "retirement," in my case, have to be taken with a grain of salt. How is it "work" to observe and comment on sports? And if one's life was all work and all play, as I am claiming about myself, how does one retire from it? The distinctions just don't make sense. All I can say is it has been a wonderful life being in the media and covering the outrageous world of sports. Oh, and if you'll pardon me, it's playoff time in football right now, and I have to watch a big game between the Indianapolis Colts and the New England Patriots.

Index

Aaron, Hank, 110, 160
ABC, 129, 201, 202
Abel, Sid, 83
Abofs, Harry, 41
Adams, Jack, 82
Adams, Weston, 96
Allen, Ralph, 196
All-Star Game [baseball]: (1951) 154; (1956) 155; (1991) 156, 168
Alomar, Roberto, 170
Ameche, Allen, 138
American Football League (AFL), 130, 131, 136
American League Baseball, 110, 154, 165–166, 167
American League Championships, 167, 170
Amsterdam Games (1928), 148
Anne, Princess, 15–16
Archer, George, 182
Arctic Club (Vancouver), 53
Argonaut Rowing Club, 41
Arizona, 156, 198
Art Ross Trophy, 92
Ash, Gord, 171
Astrodome (Houston), 132
Athens Games (2004), 148
Atlanta Braves, 170
Atlanta Games (1996), 147–148
Augusta National [Golf Club], 107, 174, 175, 183–184, 193
Ault, Doug, 166–167

Babashoff, Shirley, 145
Bailey, Donovan, 147–148
Ballard, Harold, 67, 73–74, 76–77, 84–85, 119–127

Ballard, Yolanda, 122–123, 127
Ballesteros, Seve, 185
Baltimore Colts, 130, 131, 138–139
Baltimore Orioles, 152
Banks, Ernie, 110
Bannister, Roger, 203
Barbara Lynn (cruiser), 97
Barrow, John, 54
Baseball Hall of Fame, 156, 159
Bassett, John, 33, 34, 35–36, 40, 165, 192
Bauer, Father David, 70
Bavasi, Peter, 167
Bawel, Bibbles, 52
B.C. Lions, 31
Beach, Orm, 44
Beauchamp, Jacques, 21
Beddoes, Dick, 44, 78–79, 119, 125, 196–197
Beeston, Paul, 167, 170
Belichick, Bill, 136
Beliveau, Jean, 86–88, 94, 105
Bell, George, 158, 169, 170
Bell, Marilyn, 6
Belmont Stakes (Kentucky Derby), 118
Berlin Games (1936), 108
Bikila, Abebe, 143
Bird, Larry, 100
Black Muslims, 64, 67
Blackout policy, 204, 205
Blake, Toe, 24
Blood doping, 146 (*See also* Drug testing; Steroids)
Bobby Hull (Hunt), 92, 93
Bolt, Tommy, 174
Bonds, Barry, 110, 160

Index

Bossy, Mike, 27
Boston Braves, 152
Boston Bruins, 20, 24–25, 26, 94–96, 97, 98–99, 104
Boston Celtics, 100
Boston Garden, 96, 100
Boston Record—American, 96
Boston Red Sox, 152, 164
Bourque, Raymond, 102
Bradshaw, Terry, 133, 138
Brehl, Jack, 17
Brezhnev, Leonid, 72–73, 79
Bright, Johnny, 50
British Amateur Championship, 107
British Open, 107, 173, 177, 180, 183, 184, 186
Brochu, Claude, 164
Bronfman, Charles, 162–163, 164
Bronfman, Sam, 163
Brooklyn Dodgers, 109–110, 159, 162, 163
Bruno, Frank, 68
Brunt, Stephen, 199–201
Bryant, Bear, 33, 131
Buckner, Bill, 152
Buffalo Bills, 134, 135–137
Burton, Sophia, 60, 61, 62

Cahill, Leo, 39, 40
Calgary Flames, 93
Calgary Games (1988), 149
Calgary Herald, 200
Calgary Stampeders, 32, 46
Campbell, Clarence, 19, 20–21, 22–23, 71
Canada AM (CTV), 2
Canada Cup: (1976), 99; (1987), 105 (*See also* Team Canada)
Canada–Russia hockey series (1972/1974), 69–80, 98, 195, 196–197, 203
Canadian Football League (CFL), 29, 30, 34, 36, 137, 193, 200, 205
Canadian Imperial Bank of Commerce (CIBC), 166
Canadian Olympic Federation, 207
Canadian Open, 174, 179, 183, 187
Canadian Press, 20

Carnoustie (Scotland), 180
Carpentier, Georges, 113
Carter, Gary, 163
Carter, Joe, 170, 171
Casey, Tom, 48
Catherwood, Ethel, 148
CBC, 75, 198, 202, 206
CBS: radio, 2; TV, 129
CFRB (radio), 71
Champions Dinner (Masters), 181, 182, 183
CHCH (TV), 120
Cheek, Tom, 171
Cherry, Don, 74, 196
Chesler, Lou, 138–139
Chicago Bears, 35, 46
Chicago Blackhawks, 89–90, 91–92, 98, 115
Chicago Cardinals, 31
Chicago Cubs, 156, 198
Chicago Tribune, 194
Chicago White Sox, 166, 168
Churchill Downs (Louisville), 192
Chuvalo, George, 67–68
Cincinnati Reds, 157
Citytv, 198
CKEY (radio), 2
Clair, Frank, 33
Clancy, King, 122
Clarke, Bobby, 73, 74
Clay, Cassius Marcellus (boxer), 58–59, 60–63, 64, 67 (*See also* Muhammad Ali; Sonny Liston–Cassius Clay fight)
Clay, Cassius Marcellus (slaveowner), 64–65
Clay, Rudolph, 60
Clemens, Roger, 171
Closed circuit television, 65
CNE Stadium (Toronto), 34, 38, 54, 165
Cochrane, Mickey, 156
Cole, Bob, 195
Cole, Eric, 8
Coleman, Jim, 79, 191, 196
Colour barrier, 109–110 (*See also* Racism; Slavery)
Comaneci, Nadia, 145–146
Communist Party, 73

Index

Competitiveness, 2–3
Computers, 3–4
Conacher, Charlie, 115, 116
Conacher, Lionel, 107, 115–116
Cook, Bun, 91
Cooke, Jack, 165
Cosell, Howard, 201–202
Cox, Bobby, 170
Craig, Gordon, 206–207
Crawford, Hasely, 146
Creighton, Doug, 52
Crichton, Hec, 46
Crosby, Bing, 182
Crosby, Sidney, 105
Cross–dressing athlete, 149
Crothers, Bill, 142, 143
Csonka, Larry, 132
CTV network, 2, 73, 192, 195
Cuba, 146
Cy Young Award, 164, 171

Daley, Arthur, 67
Dallas Cheerleaders, 134
Dallas Cowboys, 133–134, 136–137
Davis, Al, 136
Davis, Bill, 169
Davis, Howard, 146
Dawson, Andre, 163
Deep South, 174
Delormier Downs (Montreal), 47
Dempsey, Jack, 112–115
Denver Broncos, 134, 135
Detroit Lions, 35, 36, 204
Detroit Red Wings, 16, 17, 21, 22,
    24, 82–83, 84, 90, 91, 94
Detroit Tigers, 153, 154, 156–157,
    168
DiMaggio, Joe, 14–15, 151, 153,
    154, 155, 156, 157
DiManno, Rosie, 145
Disney, Walt, 156
Drapeau, Jean, 22
Drug testing, 146, 147–148
Dryden, Ken, 27
Drylie, Bill, 16
Dundee, Angelo, 63
Dunedin (Florida), 166
Dunnell, Milt, 2, 22, 67, 187, 191–193

Duplessis, Maurice, 80
Durocher, Leo, 160

Eagleson, R. Alan, 75–76, 94–97, 98
East York Lyndhursts, 69
Eaton, Lady, 194
Edmonton Eskimos, 30, 40, 48, 49,
    50–51, 115, 124
Edmonton Oil Kings, 95
Edmonton Oilers, 26–27, 101, 102
Edmonton Sun, 101
Eisenhower, Dwight D., 176
Elizabeth II, Queen of England,
    15–16, 118, 144
Ellis, Ron, 73
Elway, John, 135
E-mail, 3–4
Emms, Hap, 94–97
Empire Games (1954), 203
Empire Stadium (Vancouver), 52
Endorsements, 85, 110, 146
ESPN, 206
Esposito, Phil, 71, 74, 93
Etcheverry, Sam, 50
Ethiopia, 143
Exhibition Stadium (Toronto), 166

Fairly, Ron, 162
Faldo, Nick, 177, 185
Faloney, Bernie, 39, 54
The Fan 590 (radio), 2, 207
Fantasy sports, 205
Farm system, 164
Fenway Park (Boston), 162
Ferguson, Elmer, 25
Fernandez, Tony, 170
Fetchit, Stepin, 65
Finland, 76, 146
Firpo, Luis, 113–114
Fleck, Jack, 180
Fleischer, Nat, 66
Floral (Sask.), 82
Florida Marlins, 164
Fog Bowl (1962), 54–55
Fontinato, Lou, 83
Foreman, George, 192
Foxx, Jimmy, 155
Frazer, Joe, 147

Index

Free agency, 164
Frewin, Bob, 49
Fuhr, Grant, 101

Gainey, Bob, 27
Gardner, Ray, 62
Gaston, Cito, 169, 170, 171
Gaudeur, Jake, 39–40, 53
Gehrig, Lou, 152, 153
Geoffrion, Boom Boom, 23, 27, 87, 88–89
Getty, Don, 51
Gibbons, Tommy, 113
Gilchrist, Chester Carlton (Cookie), 36–37
Gillick, Pat, 167, 169, 170, 171, 172
Givens, Alex, 5
Glen Abbey (Oakville, Ont.), 179
Globe and Mail, The, 7, 8, 13, 44, 79, 191, 194, 196–197, 199
Godfrey, Paul, 137–138, 166
Gordie Howe Day, 84
Goulet, Robert, 65
Grand Slam of Golf, 180
Grange, Red, 112
Granite Club (Toronto), 48
Grant, Bud, 51–52, 54, 132, 135
Great Depression, 44
Green Bay Packers, 47, 129, 130, 204
Gregory, Jim, 125
Gretzky, Wayne, xii, 19, 25, 81, 82, 93, 97, 100–104, 105
Grey Cup, 1, 135, 200; (1921) 115; (1928) 197; (1933) 29–30; (1934) 44; (1935) 48; (1942) 45; (1948) 46; (1950) 46; (1952) 30, 203; (1953) 48, 49; (1954) 49–50; (1955) 50–51, 193; (1956) 51; (1958) 52; (1962) 54–55; (1965) 65; (1971) 40; (1983) 41; (1986) 124–125; (1992) 45
Gross, George, 194–195
Gulfstream Park (Florida), 117

Hall, Glenn, 98
Halls of fame: baseball, 156, 159; golf, 188; hockey, 84, 92, 96, 98, 123
Hamilton Spectator, 37
Hamilton Tiger-Cats, 39, 40, 47, 48, 49, 51–52, 53–54, 55, 123, 124

Hanson, Fritzie, 44
Harmon, Tom, 201
Harrington, Ed, 39
Hart Memorial Trophy, 92
Hartford Whalers, 84
Harvey, Doug, 84, 87
Hasek, Dominik, 102
Hayes, Bob, 142
Hayman, Lew, 33–34, 35, 45
Helsinki (Finland), 76–77, 78–79
Hemingway, Ernest, 9
Henderson, Hollywood, 133
Henderson, Paul, xi, 73–74, 75, 195
   (*See also* Canada–Russia hockey series)
Henderson, Rickey, 171
Henke, Tom, 170
Hewitt, Foster, 195–196, 206
Hewitt, W.A., 195
Hialeah Park (Florida), 117
Hindmarsh, Harry, 9
Hiroshima, 142
Hitler, Adolph, 108–109, 111
Hockey Hall of Fame, 84, 92, 96, 98, 123
Hockey Night in Canada, 195
Hockey riots (March 17, 1955), 21–23
   (*See also* Richard, Maurice "Rocket")
Hodge, Dave, 120
Hogan, Ben, 108, 179–182, 186, 189
Horton, Tim, 91
Houston Aeros, 84
Howe, Colleen, 78, 85–86
Howe, Gordie, 1, 16, 77–78, 81, 82–86, 87, 89, 93, 94, 105
Howe, Mark, 77, 78, 82, 84, 86
Howe, Marty, 77, 78, 82, 84, 86
Howitt, Eaton, 37
Hull, Bobby, 70–71, 77, 79, 88–93, 94, 95, 105
Hull, Brett, 25, 92–93
Hull, Joanne, 92, 93
Humeniuk, Scotty, 12
Humphrey, Dave, 52
Hungerford, George, 142
Hunt, Andrew, 78
Hunt, Caroline, 11, 17, 49, 53, 74, 121, 193–194
Hunt, Don, 3
Hunt, Kathryn, 121

Index

Hunt, Lamar, 129
Hutchinson, Fred, 154

Imlach, Punch, 86, 87, 125, 196
Imperials (Sarnia), 29
Indianapolis Colts, 207
Innsbruck Games (1976), 194
Instant replay, 205
International League Baseball, 109
Internet, 205
Irvin, Dick, 20
Ismail, Rocket, 41
Israeli athletes, massacre, 141, 143, 144
Ivan, Tommy, 90
Ivor Wynne Stadium (Hamilton), 124

Jackson, Janet, 137
Jackson, Roger, 142
Jackson, Russ, 39
Jacobs, Indian Jack, 46–47, 48
Jamaica, 146
James, Norm, 9
Jarry Park (Montreal), 161–162
Jenner, Bruce, 146
Jerome, Harry, 142
Johnson, Ben, 147, 199
Johnson, Eddie, 104
Jonas, Don, 40
Jones, Bobby, 107–108, 112, 178
Juantorena, Alberto, 146

Kansas City Chiefs, 129
Kansas City Royals, 167
Kashower, Bob, 50
Kearns, Jack (Doc), 113
Kelly, Jim, 137
Kelly, Red, 87–88
Kemper Lakes (Chicago), 176
Kennedy, Ethel, 134
Kennedy, John F., 14
Kennedy, Robert, 134
Kennedy, Ted, 83
Kennedy Space Center (Florida), 188
Kentucky Derby (1964), 116–117
    (See also Belmont Stakes; Preakness;
    Triple Crown)
KGB (Soviet secret police), 77, 79
Kharlamov, Valery, 71, 74, 76–77
Kidd, Bruce, 142

Kiick, Jim, 132
Kingsbury, Jim, 49
Knox, Ronnie, 34–35
Knudson, George, 182–183
Korean War, 154
Kwong, Normie, 50

Labatt Blue, 166
Labatt Brewing Co., 165, 166
Lach, Elmer, 24
Lady Wonder, 49
Lafleur, Guy, 27
Lambton Golf & Country Club
    (Toronto), 189
Landy, John, 203
Langer, Bernhard, 184
Laycoe, Hal, 20
Layne, Bobby, 36
Lear, Les, 47
Lemieux, Claude, 25
Lemieux, Mario, 19, 81, 100, 104–105
Leonard, Stan, 175–176, 182
Leonard, "Sugar" Ray, 146
Levy, Marv, 135
Lewis, Lennox, 147
Lewiston (Maine), 64, 65
Liberal Party of Canada, 116
Life magazine, 83
Lincoln, Abraham, 65
Lindbergh, Charles, 9
Lindros, Eric, 94, 96, 105
Lindsay, Ted, 16, 17, 83
Liske, Peter, 40
Liston, Sonny, xi, 57, 58, 60, 61,
    63–66, 68, 131, 135 (See also Sonny
    Liston—Cassius Clay fight; Sonny
    Liston—Floyd Patterson fight; Sonny
    Liston—Muhammad Ali fight)
London Hunt Club (London, Ont.),
    187
Loria, Jeffrey, 164
Los Angeles Games: (1932) 148–149;
    (1984) 147
Los Angeles Kings, xii, 41, 101–102
LPGA, 188

McCabe, Eddie, 78–79
McCallum, Hiram (Buck), 46
McDonald, Ab, 89

Index

McDonald, Lanny, 200
McDougall, Don, 166
McDougall, Gerry, 54
McGill University (Montreal), 144
McGrady, Tracy, 206
McGriff, Fred, 170
McKenzie, Ada, 188–189
McNall, Bruce, 41, 102
McNaughton, Dunc, 149
McQuay, Leon, 41
MacDonald, John, 17
Mahovlich, Frank, 71, 72, 90
Mailer, Norman, 58–59
Major League Baseball, 164, 165
Manley, Dexter, 135
Mann, Dave, 37, 39
Mantle, Micky, xi, 1, 89, 153,
    157–159, 178
Maple Leaf Gardens (Toronto),
    16–18, 67, 71, 77, 84, 85, 90, 91,
    95, 98, 120, 124, 125
Marciano, Rocky, 63–54
Maris, Roger, 89, 151, 157, 158, 159,
    178
Martinez, Pedro, 164
Masks (hockey), 92
Masters Golf Championship, 107–108,
    173–176, 178–179, 180, 181, 182,
    182, 185, 186, 193
Mays, Willie, 110, 159–160
Media (sports), 191–207
Meeker, Howie, 78–79, 90
Memorial Cup, 95, 104
Miami Dolphins, 132
Michigan Wolverines, 201
Middlecoff, Cary, 175–176, 180
Mike Tyson—Frank Bruno fight
    (1989), 68
Mikhailov, Boris, 78
Miles, Rollie, 48
Milne, Veronica, 122, 123
Minnesota Twins, 170
Minnesota Vikings, 132, 134, 135
Minter, Cedric, 41
Missouri State Prison, 59
Mize, Larry, 185
Monahan, Leo, 96
Monday, Rick, 163

Monroe, Marilyn, 14–15
Montana, Joe, 135, 138
Montreal Alouettes, 36, 47, 50–51,
    135, 144
Montreal Canadiens, 23, 24–25, 27,
    86–88, 91, 93, 94, 102, 125, 126,
    146
Montreal Expos, 144, 161–165
    (*See also* Washington Nationals)
Montreal Forum, 19–23, 26
Montreal Games (1976), 2, 15–16,
    143–147
Montreal Gazette, 20, 69
Montreal Maroons, 115
Montreal Matin, 21
Montreal Royals, 109
Montreal Star, 25
Moore, Archie, 58
Morrall, Earl, 131
Morris, Jack, 170
Mosca, Angelo, 38
Moscow. *See* Canada–Russia hockey series
Mount Royal Hotel (Montreal), 47–48
Mud Bowl (1950, Varsity Stadium), 46
Muhammad Ali, xi, 1, 57–68, 115,
    131, 135, 147, 192, 200, 202
Mulroney, Brian, 156
Munich Games (1972), 141, 143, 144
Musial, Stan, 159

Namath, Joe, 130–132, 133, 138
National Film Board, 200
National Football League (NFL), 31,
    33, 34, 35, 36, 40, 41, 43, 46, 47,
    50, 129, 130, 133, 137, 138,
    203–204, 205
National Hockey League (NHL), 19,
    21, 70, 71, 74, 77, 84, 88, 89, 90,
    91, 94, 97, 101, 102, 115
National League Baseball, 110
National Newspaper Awards, 13
Nazi Germany, 108, 111
Neilson, Roger, 125–126
New England Patriots, 137, 207
New England Whalers, 84 (*See also*
    Hartford Whalers)
New York Giants, 50, 134, 135–136,
    138, 159–160, 204

Index

New York Islanders, 27, 126

New York Jets, 130, 131–132

New York Mets, 152, 160

New York Rangers, 23, 82, 83, 87, 90, 101, 102, 202

New York Times, The, 67, 132, 194

New York Yankees, xi, 151, 152–153, 156, 157–159, 163, 167, 169

New Zealand, 142

News Radio National Network, 2

Newsome, Buck, 157

NFL Sunday Ticket, 205

NHL lockout (2004–2005), 102

Niagara Falls, 14

Nicholson, Jack, 173

Nicklaus, Jack, 108, 173, 177–179, 183, 184

Nicklaus, Jackie (Jack's son), 179

No, No, Nanette, 152

Norman, Greg, 185–186

Norman, Moe, 186–188

Noronic (ship), 11–13

Northern Dancer, 116–118, 192

Norwood, Scott, 136

Oakland A's, 170, 171

Oakland Hills (Detroit), 189–190

Oakland Raiders, 130, 131, 136

Obodiac, Stan, 125

"O Canada," 72

O'Connor, Zeke, 31

O'Meara, Baz, 20

O'Quinn, Red, 50

Olympic Stadium (Montreal), 143–144, 162, 165

Olympics, 2: (1936) 108; (1960), 58; (1976) 2, 15–16, 143–147, 194, 201; (1988), 149; (2002) 103, 105; (2010) 149 (*See also* Summer Olympics; Games under name of host city)

Ontario Ladies' Championship (golf), 188–189

Ontario Open, 186

Ontario Rugby Football Union (ORFU), 29

Orange Bowl Stadium (Miami), 133

Order of Canada, 125

Ornest, Harry, 41

Orr, Bobby, 1, 81–82, 93–100, 101, 104, 106

Orr, Doug, 95–97

Oshawa Generals, 94, 95, 97

Ottawa Journal, 78

Owens, Jesse, 107, 108–109

Pal Hal (Beddoes), 119

Palmer, Arnold, 1, 108, 173, 174–178, 179, 184

Pan American Games (1967), 206–207

Parent, Bernie, 85

Paris, Bubba, 135

Paris (Ont.), 8–9

Parker, Jackie, 50–51

Patrick, Lester, 82

Patrick, Lynn, 97–98

Patterson, Floyd, 57, 59

Patterson, Harold, 50

Pay-per-view, 204–205

Penman's plant (Paris, Ont.), 8–9

Penticton V's, 69–70

Percival Molson Memorial Stadium (Montreal), 144

Perry, Norm, 30

PGA Championships, 175, 176, 180, 183, 186

Phantom punch, xi, 65 (*See also* Muhammad Ali)

Phelan, T.N., 10

Philadelphia Eagles, 52

Philadelphia Flyers, 84, 85, 104

Philadelphia Phillies, 171

Phoenix Coyotes, 103

Piniella, Lou, 169

Pittsburgh Penguins, 104, 105

Pittsburgh Pirates, 152

Pittsburgh Steelers, 132–134, 138

Plante, Jacques, 91

Ploen, Kenny, 54

Pocklington, Peter, 101, 102

Polo Grounds (NY), 113, 159

Pool, Hamp, 34, 35

Port Arthur (Ont.), 11

Port Credit (Ont.), 11

Preakness (Kentucky Derby), 118

Prime Time Sports, 2, 207

Index

Proudfoot, Jim, 193–194
Puerto Rico, 161

Quarrie, Donald, 146
Quarrington, Nelson, 13
Quebec Aces, 86
Quebec Nordiques, 96
Queen's Park (press gallery), 2
Queen's University, 197

Racism, 48, 109–110, 111, 173–174, 183
Raymond, Senator Donat, 86
RCAF Hurricanes, 45
Reddish, Willie, 66
Reese, Pee Wee, 110
Reeve, Ted, 55, 197–198
Reynolds, Jim, 38
Ricciardi, J.P., 172
Rice, Jerry, 135
Rice Stadium (Houston), 132
Richard, Maurice "Rocket," 1, 19–27, 81, 87, 88, 89, 91, 193
(*See also* Hockey riots)
Rickey, Branch, 109–110
Rider Cup, 189
Ring Magazine, 66
Ripken, Cal, Jr., 152
Rivera golf course (California), 174
Roberts, Clifford, 175–176
Robertson, John, 169
Robertson, Roy, 50
Robinson, Jackie, 107, 109–110
Robinson, Larry, 27
Rogers Centre, 172 (*See also* SkyDome)
Rogers, Steve, 162, 163
Romania, 145
Rome Games, 58, 142, 143
Rooney, Dan, 132–133
Roosevelt, Franklin D., 111
Rose Bowl (1987), 134
Rosebloom, Carroll, 138–139
Rosenfeld, Bobby, 148
Rote, Tobin, 35–37, 38
Rowe, Schoolboy, 151
Roy, Patrick, 102
Royal Canadian Golf Association, 186–187

Royal Montreal golf course, 179
Royal Oak golf course (Florida), 188
Royal Yacht Britannia, 15
Royal York Hotel (Toronto), 46
Rozelle, Peter, 132
Ruth, Babe, 112, 151–153, 155, 158, 178

St. Augustine (Florida), 188
St. Clair Weekly Bugle, 2
St. Louis Blues, 98, 102, 127
St. Louis Cardinals, 116, 154, 156, 159, 161
Sakic, Joe, 24
Salaries: baseball, 155; football, 36, 130; hockey, 82, 85, 87, 92, 94–97, 102
Salt Lake City Games (2002), 103
San Francisco 49ers, 135, 138
San Francisco Giants, 165
Sarnia (Ont.), 11, 29–30, 44, 111, 156, 201, 206
Sarnia Golf Club, 189
Sarnia Observer, 2
Saskatchewan Roughriders, 44
Schenley Award, 40, 48
Schmeling, Max, 111–112
Schmidt, Milt, 98
Seagrams, 163
Seattle Mariners, 165, 171
Secretariat, 117
(*See also* Northern Dancer)
Security, Olympics, 141, 144–145
Selke, Frank, 24
Selke, Frank, Sr., 86–87
Semenko, Dave, 101
Seoul Games (1988), 147, 199
Shanahan, Brendan, 102
Shatto, Dick, 33, 37, 38
Shaw, Bob, 31–32
Shea Stadium (NY), 152
Shelby (Montana), 113
Shore, Eddie, 96
Sifford, Charlie, 174
Simmons, Steve, 199, 200–201
Simpson, Bobby, 38
Simpson, Jimmie, 48
Sittler, Darryl, 125
Skalbania, Nelson, 101

Index

SkyDome (Toronto), 45, 168, 169, 170, 172, 204 (*See also* Rogers Centre)
Slapshot, 91–92
Slavery, 64–65
  (*See also* Colour barrier; Racism)
Smith, Jackie, 134
Smith, Paul, 17
Smythe, Conn, 21, 67, 196
Snead, Sam, 108, 181–182, 189
Snell, Peter, 142
Snider, Duke, 159
Soldier Field (Chicago), 114
Somerville, Sandy, 108
Sonny Liston—Floyd Patterson fight, 57, 63–64
Sonny Liston—Cassius Clay fight, 62–66
Sonny Liston—Muhammad Ali fight, 64–66, 131
Sonshine, Harry, 32–33
Sosa, Sammy, 168
Southern Illinois University, 168
Soviet/Canada hockey rivalry, 69–70
  (*See also* Canada–Russia hockey series)
Spears, Borden, 14
Spinks, Harold, 146
Spinks, Leon, 146
Sports Hot Seat (CTV), 192–193
Sports Illustrated, 65–66
Sportsnet, 207
Stadium Club (Yankee Stadium), 153
Stanford Stadium (California), 3
Stanley Cup Playoffs: (1950) 83; (1955) 16; (1956) 87; (1960) 87–88; (1961) 90–91; (1969) 98; (1975) 85; (1980) 101, 126; (1986) 93; (1988) 101; (1993) 102; (1998) xii; (2004) 103
"Star-Spangled Banner, The," 65
Staubach, Roger, 133, 134
Stephenson, Bill, 71
Steroids, 145, 147, 160 (*See also* Blood doping; Drug testing)
Stevenson, Teofilo, 146
Stewart, Dave, 171
Stieb, Dave, 168–169
Stirrett, Jo-Jo, 30
Storey, Red, 25

Streit, Marlene Stewart, 188–189
Strike, Hilda, 149
Strikes: covering, 8; baseball, 164, 171; NHL lockout, 102
Stukus, Annis, 31
Summer Olympics: (1928) 148; (1932) 148–149; (1964) 141–143, 202–203; (1972) 141, 143, 144; (1976) 1, 15–16, 143–147; (1984) 147; (1988) 147, 199; (1996) 147–148; (2000) 148; (2004) 148
Summit Series. *See* Canada—Russia hockey series
Sunbelt teams, 103
Super Bowl, ix, 3, 43, 103, 129–139, 193, 204
Swann, Lynn, 133
Sydney Games (2000), 148

Taylor, E.P., 116, 117, 118
TC Puck (Ballard's dog), 122, 123
Team Canada, 70–76, 80, 98
  (*See also* Canada–Russia hockey series)
Television, 20, 103, 198–207
Terrell, Ernie, 67
Theismann, Joe, 39, 40
Thomas, Thurman, 136
Thompson, Jim, 206–207
Thunder Bay (Ballard cottage), 122, 123
Tickets
  baseball, 172
  football, 45, 137
Tiger Stadium (Detroit), 154
Tinsley, Buddy, 46
Titanic, 186
Titleist, 188
Tokyo Games (1964), 141–143, 202–203
Toronto Argonauts, 3, 18, 29–42, 46, 49, 115, 124, 137, 165, 192
Toronto Blue Jays, 137, 161, 162, 163, 165, 166–172, 204
Toronto Islands, 11
Toronto Maple Leafs, 16, 21, 26, 73, 74, 76, 83, 84–85, 86, 88, 90, 102, 119, 120, 123, 124, 125–127, 195, 196, 204–205, 206

Index

Toronto Raptors, 206
Toronto Star, 1, 2, 3, 5–18, 20, 22, 30, 31–32, 34, 37, 48–49, 52, 67, 116, 125, 145, 187, 188, 191, 193, 194, 195
Toronto Star Weekly, 2, 88, 202
Toronto Sun, 2, 38, 52, 101, 122, 137, 169, 173, 183, 186, 191, 194–195, 197, 199, 200, 207
Toronto Telegram, 3, 6, 7, 13, 33, 34, 49, 52, 165, 192, 194, 197
Trafton, George, 46–47
Trevino, Lee, 183–184, 186
Trimble, Jim, 51–52, 53–54
Trinidad, 146
Triple Crown: baseball, 158; horse racing, 118
Troyer, Fred, 12
Trudeau, Pierre, 88, 162–163
TSN, 206–207
Tunney, Gene, 114–115
Tyson, Mike, 68

Unitas, Johnny, 131, 138, 139
University of Kentucky, 33
University of Michigan, 84
University of Western Ontario, 1, 5, 12, 79, 187, 199
U.S. Amateurs Championship, 107, 189
U.S. Open, 107, 173, 174, 176–177, 178, 179–180, 183, 189
Ussery, Bobby, 117

Vancouver Games (2010), 149
Vancouver Sun, 196
Varsity Stadium (Toronto), 32, 34, 45, 46, 49, 142
Velez, Otto "the Swatto," 167
Vero Beach (Florida), 110, 196–197
Vessels, Billy, 48
Vienna (Austria), 70
Vietnam War, 66–67
Vijuk, Joe, 40
Violence in hockey, 74, 78, 83
Viren, Lasse, 146

Waite, Hoyt, 153
Walasiewicz, Stella, 149
Walcott, Jersey Joe, 66

Walker, Larry, 164
Wall, Art, 175
Wallace, Stan, 39
Ward, Duane, 170
Washington Nationals, 144, 161
Washington Redskins, 40, 134
Washington Senators, 155, 165
Webster, Alex, 50
Webster, R. Howard, 166
Weir, Mike, 182
Weiss, George, 158
Weisskopf, Tom, 179
Werblin, Sonny, 130
Weston Golf Club (Toronto), 174, 175
Wharnsby, Tim, 173
Whitfield, Simon, 148
Wide World of Sports, 202
Williams, Brian, 75, 198–199
Williams, Doug, 134–135
Williams, Jimy, 169
Williams, Percy, 148, 149
Williams, Ted, 26, 151, 153, 154–156, 160
Wilson, Bob, 90
Wilson, Ralph, 136
Windsor (Ont.), 13–14
Windfields Farm (Oshawa, Ont.), 118
Winnipeg Blue Bombers, 44, 46, 47, 48, 51–52, 53–55, 135
Winnipeg Jets, 92
Wirkowski, Nobby, 30
Woods, Tiger, 1, 173, 177, 179, 180
World Cup (hockey, 2004), 102, 105
World Golf Hall of Fame, 188
World Hockey Association (WHA), 70, 74, 77–79, 82, 84–85, 88, 92
World Hockey Championships, 69–71, 76–79
World Series, 152, 154, 156–157, 159, 162, 163, 167–168, 169, 170, 171
World War I, 113
World War II, 45, 89, 111–112, 154

Yakushev, Alexander, 71, 76
Yankee Stadium, xi, 65, 111, 153
Young, Scott, 196

Zaleski, Joe, 47
Znaimer, Moses, 199

About the Author

Jim Hunt was born and raised in Sarnia, Ontario. He graduated in 1948 from the newly established journalism course at
the University of Western Ontario, and in fact was a member
of the very first graduating class. He joined the *Toronto Star*
in general and political reporting, transferring to sports in
1953, under the legendary Milt Dunnell. It was all sports the
rest of the way for Hunt: sports editor at the *Star Weekly*;
news and sports director at radio station CKEY; ten years as
co-host of the nationally syndicated *Prime Time Sports* on
the FAN590, where he still appears on the morning show;
and a regular panelist on CTV's *Canada AM*. Since 1983,
he has been a sports columnist for the *Toronto Sun*, for whom
he still writes a regular weekly column. In 2001, he received
the Achievement Award from Sports Media Canada.